Golfer's Start-Up:

A Beginner's Guide to Golf
2nd Edition

By Doug W

Start-Up Sports® **#7**

TRACKS

Tracks Publishing
San Diego, California

Golfer's Start-Up
A Beginner's Guide to Golf
2nd Edition
By Doug Werner

Tracks Publishing
140 Brightwood Avenue
Chula Vista, CA 91910
(619) 476-7125
www.trackspublishing.com

Start-Up Sports®

Copyright © 2010 by Doug Werner
10 9 8 7 6 5 4 3 2 1

Cataloging-in-Publication Data

Werner, Doug, 1950-

    Golfer's start-up : a beginner's guide to golf / by Doug Werner. -- 2nd ed. -- San Diego, Calif. : Tracks Pub., c2010.

        p. ; cm.
        (Start-up sports ; #7)

        ISBN: 978-1-884654-76-3
        Previous edition: 1996.
        Includes bibliographical references and index.

        1. Golf--Amateurs' manuals. 2. Golf--Handbooks, manuals, etc.
    I. Title. II. Series.

GV965 .W47 2010   2010934312
796.352--dc22   1010

Dedicated to

Tom Dailey
Patrick Marlborough
John Carroll
Rudi Southerland
Jaime Rae Sandoval

You have made my game
and the production of this book a remarkably
pleasant and productive experience.

Thank you!

Acknowledgements

Richard Penner
Bob Zabaronick
Tom Morton
Mark "Sook" Suchomel
Kathleen Wheeler
Dave Recker
Mr. Earl
Mark Nobel
Lynn's Photo
ColorType
Fred Stewart
Tom Komin
Gloria Sandoval
Jimmy Sandoval
Tim Fox
Red Werner
Ann Werner
Cheryl Haab
Bookcrafters
Gene Wheeler
Genie Wheeler
Ron Brady
Phyllis Carter
Ted Jackson
Jim Clinkscales

Tom Dailey
Patrick Marlborough
John Carroll
Rudi Southerland
Jaime Rae Sandoval

Bill Stewart
Henry Ford

Mission Start-Up

This book lays it out for the beginner who wants to learn how to *move the ball along.* How to hit the ball well enough to get out there and play a few rounds. *Golfer's Start-Up* is simple, easy to read and light in spirit. Its *intent* is to connect with the unskilled player unfamiliar with the sometimes confusing culture of golf. A culture that loves its language and its many explanations for doing things. I wrote it during my own learning experiences so it has a greenhorn's point of view that should ring true with most beginners and everyone else who cares to remember their first clumsy and frustrating days.

The first half of the book is instructional and the last part is an accounting of my own golfing education. Obviously, it's not a Celebrity Golfer's Diatribe, however, in its own stumbling and endearing way, that is probably its greatest strength. If nothing else, beginners will find solace, hopefully a few laughs and not a bad angle on the ancient art of stroking the little white ball.

Golf is a difficult game to learn (writing this book was easier) but that doesn't mean it has to be blood, sweat and tears. With the right attitude it's alotta fun. Even in the beginning.

Doug Werner

Contents

Contents

Why Play?

It's So-oh Stupid

Although enjoyed by millions, many folks can't understand the lure of golf. Of all the reasons I've heard about why folks don't play, this one seems to pop out more than most:

"It just seems so stupid. Walking around all day and trying to hit a little ball into a hole."

And who can argue with that? I certainly won't.

Seems so stupid? Sure does. Sometimes it seems even more stupid when you've played awhile.

Walking around all day? Seems like it. Eighteen holes takes about four hours on a *good* day.

Hitting a little ball? Indeed. A difficult thing to do at all, let alone properly.

Into a hole? Impossible! It's hard enough to just *hit* the bloody ball, let alone *aim* it at a target.

So I agree. I guess that's why I didn't play as a younger person. Too many really cool things to try instead. Like surfing or mountain bike riding or snowboarding. Golfing was just so *uninspiring* compared to the action sports. Hard to do and just sorta blah, you know?

Betcha Can't Hit Just One

Despite all that, if you can hit *just one ball* so soundly ...

... that you finally feel the lovely crush of ball against sweetspot,

... so that the fullness and *fineness* of that honeyed hit glides through your hands, arms, shoulders and back like something erotic and faintly electric,

... and as a result the ball takes a long and soaring, straight and mighty path toward the target ...

it's a *certainty* that you'll want to hit another.

<u>*That*</u> is The Basic Lure of Golf.

Sweetness — Smacking it on the button and sending it long, straight and true is heady stuff. It's the quest, the pleasure and the addiction of golf.

The Social Connection

Golf is a common denominator among a giant swath of humanity. A unique one in that all golfers find the game fascinating if not compelling. It's a wonder, it's a lark, it's a challenge and it's a laugh. Nothing else is quite the same and nothing else animates an encounter quite like golf. Even if it's just a conversation about golf.

Golfers love to talk golf. They love to share advice. They love to talk about the great shots and the lousy shots. They love to connect with each other through the game. I've surfed and skied and snowboarded and sailed and skated and enjoyed all kinds of other things, but it's golf that reigns when the jawing begins.

In other words it's a great way to spend time with people. Through play or conversation.

A Physical Game

Contrary to what some may think, golf is good exercise if you walk the course. Eighteen holes is maybe five miles of brisk walking. I've played jogging between shots and that, as you can imagine, is quite a workout.

Golf is also played outside in an attractive or downright beautiful setting that opens the heart and mind among those of us who spend so much time in enclosed spaces.

A challenging physical effort it ain't, but then again, it's not billiards either. Stay off the carts and move at a good clip, and you'll get some exercise.

A Thinking Game

No doubt about that. Golf demands thought, concentration and focus. You gotta think about the lie, or setting, of the ball, which club to use, how to use it and even the weather every time you address the ball. The variables come at you from all directions.

If nothing else, golf is always a mental challenge. And like meeting any mental challenge, it's a tasty thrill when you master the demands of a particular shot and place it just so.

A Real Character Builder

Don't laugh.

A good golfer has a finely developed sense of patience, fortitude and discipline. You simply cannot progress without them. Everybody hits a lousy shot. Nobody hits perfectly. **Golf is not a game of perfection. It's a game of recovery.** It's what you do *after* a bad shot or a series of poor shots that counts. To rise above a miserable performance, you need to pull yourself together, and that calls for the kind of resolution that you bring to your career and your important relationships.

It's called guts.

A Tempting Alternative — When it all goes to pot out there (and it will), losing your temper is the easiest thing to do. But golf is a game that rewards composure and numerous gut checks.

It's Fun

Early in my learning days, I was kindly informed of a certain golfing truism. It was a late summer afternoon and I was charging by myself through nine holes trying to beat the sun going down. I ran into a couple of fellows around the fifth hole who were moving kinda slow and I offered to play along with them instead of waiting or shooting on through. Like so many golfers do, they said *sure!* and we proceeded together.

Somewhere along the next hole I muffed a shot and I threw a little fit. Something like, "Ahh Doug! You can do better than that!" Nothing nasty but my displeasure was rather evident.

One of my new partners was standing next to me during the shot, and as we walked on he said, "Last Sunday an old-timer told me something that stuck with me. I wasn't playing very well and I guess it showed a little. He said, 'Golf is the only thing in life where you can have fun on a bad day.' It's something I like to keep in mind because it's so true, don't you think?"

I looked at my lousy lie, looked over the empty fairways, so pretty in the waning light, looked over at my new friend and I was struck by his easy manner. He was chuckling as he told the story and I knew he meant no harm. Only relating what came to mind in the natural way of someone at ease with himself, the surroundings and ... me.

My frustration faded immediately. I realized that underneath all my charging and grim intentions to get better,

that I was having fun despite myself. Yeah. Really
having fun after all. And that it was great to meet up
with these two guys to share the game and the cama-
raderie, and I told him so.

It's easy to get wound up with the difficulties in
playing and, being the competitive creatures that we
are, easy to form expectations of how we should play.
But it's the joy of playing that underlies all that ...

We play golf because golf is fun.

The Start

Going Mental

It's important to realize up front that golf is not an easy game to master.

Only the anointed ever swing and hit the ball consistently well from the git go. Everyone else climbs a very long and arduous learning curve. Just ask anyone who plays.

This shouldn't be a turn off. There is nothing wrong with learning something slowly as long as you *expect* the learning to be slow. The legendary frustrations associated with the game can be avoided in large part if you expect your expertise to come in bits and pieces over the long haul. Once you've rid yourself of expectations of how you *should* perform, you can begin to learn and really have fun.

Along with accepting golf's peculiar learning curve, it's also important to understand that golf requires focus. When you play and practice you must learn to concentrate and involve yourself completely with each swing. Again, this shouldn't be a turn off. When you develop concentration, it's like creating your own little world. It's a place where nothing bothers you (like other people watching, noise, your other concerns, etc.) so you can relax and get down to it. Obviously, it's a very nice place to be.

Learning to pace yourself through your golfing education and learning to focus during each swing are the mental things that will see you through. You cannot rely on raw athletic prowess, brute determination or even endless hours of practice. If you aren't patient and focused, it's a given that you'll either soon quit or become a sullen, miserable wreck.

This section is first for a reason:

Properly frame your expectations and get your head straight before you touch a club. These are the mental fundamentals upon which the mechanical fundamentals are based.

Just One Club

Don't even think about buying a set of clubs.

All you need is a 5-, 6- or 7-iron for now. That's all you'll need for perhaps another 2,000 swings. Learn how to swing with one of these middle-ish irons with their generously angled clubheads (which make hitting the

Ready to Play — Patrick Marlborough is outfitted for a new life on the range. One club (5-, 6- or 7-iron), baggy clothes and sneakers. The sleek hairdo and baggy socks are optional. Don't let Mr. Casual fool you: Patrick owns a 2 handicap and learned the game on some of the oldest, most hallowed courses in golf. That's right. He's a bona fide Scottish Hellman. We're lucky he's not wearing kilts.

Home on the Range — Get used to it. This is where you belong until you can hit the little white ball.

ball easier) and you'll be on track with this golfing business. You can find such a club in any of the major superstores, new or used sporting good stores or your local pro shop. You don't have to buy a set. You can buy just the one.

Anything'll do for now, but make sure the club's grip is good if it's used. Don't worry about the nicks and scratches. It's a good idea, too, to find a club with a good-sized clubhead with a large sweetspot. Actually, most recent models have that particular quality built into them one way or another. You'll have to search your grandfather's garage to locate a club with the smaller blades of yore.

On the Range

More than likely there's a driving range nearby where you can hit golf balls. Most golf courses have one and most towns have golf courses, of course.

Consider this: every town has a bowling establishment, right? It's simply part of the Great American Landscape. There are about 7,000 bowling centers across the USA and that's a lot.

Well, hold on to your hat. There are more than 23,000 golf courses! Unless you reside smack in the middle of the Everglades or high atop Mt. Whitney, there's a course, with a driving range, near you.

But What Should I Wear?

Keep it simple for the time being. Dress casually in loose fitting clothes. Sneakers are fine. The classier

courses may have dress codes: no shorts, tank tops, sweats or T-shirts. Call ahead in order to save yourself the hassle.

Just 30 Balls

Head out to the range with your iron and find the pro shop. There you should be able to rent buckets of golf balls to hit. Buy small buckets to begin with. Sure, all the other golfers may have these huge baskets of 100 balls each, but don't buy one of those yet. Those are for golfers who know how to hit the ball consistently.

Trying to hit 100 balls now would be like trying to run a marathon before you ever ran a mile. Chances are good that 20 to 30 balls will be all you'll need or want for each session for quite some time. You're gonna swing something awful at first. You'll hit the turf, the air and *occasionally* a piece of the ball. You're gonna think hard before each swing and painstakingly analyze what happened after. This will all add up to a certain amount of physical effort and a whole lot of mental strain. Believe it or not, the 30 balls will probably wear you out.

As you improve, you can always go back for more, but the 30 ball increment is a very good pacer. If you're having a rough time, say, after five balls, it's a lot easier to see just 25 left versus 95. You see, all those balls can start to look like homework after a while. Your attitude will crash and burn and along with it, what's left of your game. Gritting it out will not work in the very

beginning because you simply don't know what you're doing. You'll just get frustrated, blow a fuse and run amok over the fairways.

Instruction

Instruction is easy to find. You can get professional lessons at a golf course, and that is a very good place to start. After all, a pro is a pro and they (should) know how to play *and* how to teach. If you click with a good one, you're on your way. If you don't, at least you're learning something from an insider and that's OK, too.

You can also get informal lessons from friends as well as from complete strangers. You will discover soon enough that golfers lurk everywhere, and all golfers love to talk about their game. Golfing is a game that very few ever get down pat, so every golfer is more or less a perpetual student. Advice and information is freely given — much like folks who suffer from the same health problem.

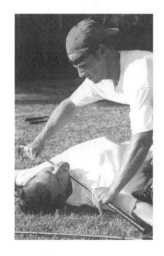

The problem with informal instruction is that it may be faulty and inconsistent. Or annoying because it's your best friend or spouse. It's wise to back up such instruction with more reliable sources. However, I've got to say right here that some of the best lessons I ever had came from a buddy.

There's also a mother lode of instruction available in books, magazines, videos and on television that can be very useful if you know how to use it and you know

what you're looking for. It's probably best to start off with in-person instruction before you tackle the material. But once you've got your feet wet, it's a great idea to do a little reading and watching. Something will click.

The thing is, this instruction stuff is very much an individual endeavor. It's also an ongoing process that really never ends. There aren't any black and white answers or steps set in stone. That's why there's so much instructional material, so many schools of thought, so many learning gizmos, and so many people telling you how to do the same thing in a dozen different ways. The trick is to sort it out your own way and to make it work for you.

It doesn't have to be confusing. Start with lessons and begin hitting the ball on the range. Develop your swing and your ability to strike the ball. After a bit you'll have a "game" with all its weaknesses and strengths and you'll begin to know what you need. Look for help as the need arises and don't be afraid to look anywhere. Use what works and filter out the rest.

The Basic Swing

Hitting the Little Ball

Golf is all about hitting the ball at a target. Either by belting it with a club or tapping it with a putter.

Putting is one thing and shouldn't be underestimated (it's often called the most important, the least practiced part of the game), but hitting a ball with a putter is a lot easier than swinging and hitting it true with a club. Sure, there are fine points and such, but even someone starting out can putt a ball. That's why there's such a thing as miniature golf. You don't miss the ball, for example, when you putt. Miss the hole, yeah, but everyone gets a piece of a putt.

Hitting golf balls expertly with woods and irons is really, really hard. It doesn't come easy and it takes awhile. It isn't like other sports or games where natural talent can see you through. Before you get any good at all, you have to master very specific fundamentals. Some are easy to learn and some are not. And there's a lot to remember. Furthermore, these basics are all connected so they pretty much have to be learned in sync. It's a little overwhelming at first.

Given that, here's the most important advice anyone can give a beginning golfer: *Be patient with your progress.* Understand right away that it won't be easy and that you'll need to invest some time. It's what I need to tell myself every time I go out there. If you let that sink in, maybe the learning process won't be such a pain in the ass. Remember: We do this kind of thing to have *fun!*, folks. So plan on doing the homework and practice, practice, practice accordingly. Not to be good immediately, *but to simply get better.*

Start with learning the following fundamentals of a sound swing. Get this stuff down. Study it like you do (or did) homework or office work. Get it into your head so you know it like you know your job or your class assignment. Learn it mentally so you never forget it.

Then practice it. I mean really practice. Do it over and over. Just like you do every day with all kinds of other stuff like job-related tasks, family-related tasks, home-making, housekeeping, yardwork, errands ... Heck, all of us spend 90 percent of our time doing things we aren't that happy about doing, so why not take the time to practice your golf swing? The upside is that it will eventually become fun, unlike most everything else you do.

Practice at the driving range. Practice with a practice ball (whiffle ball) in the park. Practice in front of a mirror. Learn the fundamentals physically as well as mentally. Learn them so they stick.

BEFORE YOU SWING

The Grip

You don't hold the handle any old which way. There's a very specific way to grip a golf club to ensure a solid and accurate stroke. These are directions for right-handers. Just reverse them if you're a lefty.

The Left Hand Does This:

Like you're shaking hands, grip the handle so that the shaft sets underneath the heel pad of your hand. Angle the shaft over your palm so that it lies over the middle joint of the index finger. Wrap the other three fingers around the handle and rest your thumb on top of the shaft.

The Right Hand Does This:

The right hand holds the club with the fingers. The shaft lies in a line from the base of the little finger to the bottom knuckle of the index finger. Wrap your fingers around the shaft and position your thumb to the left side of the handle.

Put Them Together Like This:

A) Overlap Grip

Most golfers use the overlap grip to knit their hands together. After securing the shaft with the left hand, overlap your grip with your right hand so that the little finger of the right hand nestles in between the index finger and the second finger of your left hand. Your left hand thumb should fit comfortably in the palm crease of your right hand. The crease that is formed on each

The Grip *It's easier than it looks!*

1

The butt of the club rests beneath the left palm pad and angles across the palm over the middle joint of the first finger.

2

Wrap the other three fingers around the handle and rest your thumb on top of the shaft.

3

Another view of the left hand.

4

The right hand holds the club with the fingers. The shaft lies in a line from the base of the little finger to the bottom knuckle of the index finger.

5

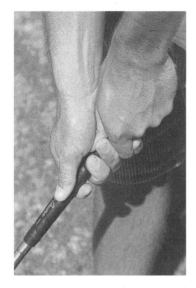

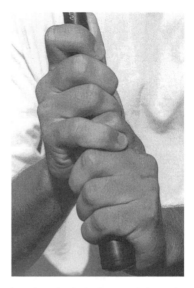

6

Overlap your grip with your right hand so that the little finger of the right hand nestles in between the index finger and the second finger of your left hand. Your left hand thumb should fit comfortably in the palm crease of your right hand. This is the overlap grip and is recommended.

7

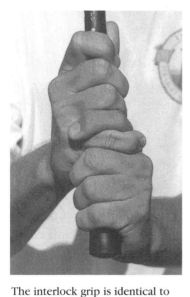

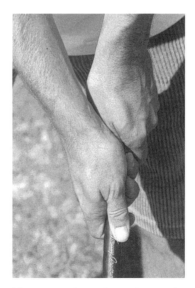

8

The interlock grip is identical to the overlap grip except that the little finger of the right hand and the index finger of the left hand intertwine.

The crease that is formed on each hand between thumb and forefinger should point toward your right ear. The right thumb rests to the left of the handle.

hand between thumb and forefinger should point toward your right ear.

B) Interlock Grip

This grip may work better for smaller hands and fingers. It is perfectly suitable, however, for anybody who feels comfy with it. The grip is identical to the overlap grip except that the little finger of the right hand and the index finger of the left hand intertwine.

Don't squeeze. Hold the club firmly without tensing your hands and forearms.

For most beginners, this is when the realization begins to dawn that golf is, indeed, *different*. After all, one doesn't grip anything else on earth with the knitted grip as described. It seems to be overly convoluted and pretentious, as if someone is pulling your leg with these instructions. But honestly, it's extremely important to grip the club exactly like this.

The knitted grip ensures that the hands will work as a cohesive unit throughout the entire swing. And once you get the grip and get used to it, it won't feel strange at all. In fact, it will become downright comfortable. You will find that the hands just sorta fold into the grip as natural as can be.

Final Pointers

The golf grip is a unique thing for a beginner to tackle. It's not just holding something. It affects the flight of every ball. ***Explore the nuances for yourself carefully.*** After all, it's your direct connection to the club and ball.

Grip gently with a touch of firmness. A death grip will hamper feel, tense you up and blister your hands.

Setting Up

Wait a minute! You don't just step up to the ball with your golfer's grip and swing away. In order to hit the ball correctly, it's very important to prepare yourself. This is pre-launch. It's time to check and set all systems. After you've pulled the trigger, stuff happens a little too fast to fiddle with.

A) Distance from the Ball

From a normal standing position, extend arms and club at chest level. Flex a bit at the knees and bend from your hips until the clubhead rests on the ground. Your spine and your clubshaft should be at right angles to each other.

A simpler and more straightforward method for guys (ladies must pretend) is to rest the clubhead on the ground and position yourself to the handle as if you're taking a whiz with it. A rather crude way to explain things, yes, (my apologies to those of you who are offended) but an effective and memorable (therefore quite useful) explanation, nevertheless.

B) Clubface and Ball Position

Place the clubhead behind the ball and square the bottom of the clubface to the target. Position your left foot in line with the ball. With your longest club (the driver), line up the ball with your left heel. As the clubs get shorter, inch your position forward. With your shortest club (the wedge), the ball should be about midway between your heels.

Determining Your Distance From the Ball

Grip your club and, from an upright standing position, extend it in front of you.

Flex your knees slightly.

Bend from the hips until the club-head rests on the turf.

That's your spot. Do it like this every time you address the ball until addressing the ball becomes second nature.

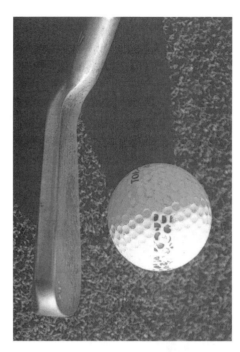

S-BOB — Or Square Blade on Ball.

This is the KEY to hitting the ball straight. You start out this way and you meet the ball this way. All the techniques and theories about hitting a golf ball have this in common.

And among the ultimate goals in golf, making sweet and square contact is the most important of all.

Ball Position
Line the ball up with your left heel when you're hitting a wood.

As the clubs descend in length, scooch yourself forward.

For the loftiest club, the sand wedge, the ball should lie on a line between your legs.

Pictured from right to left are a driver, a 5-iron and a sand wedge. Note their varied lengths as well as their different alignments.

C) Stance

Feet are shoulder-width apart for the driver. As the irons become shorter, your stance narrows. Your right foot is perpendicular to the target line, and the left points slightly out to the left.

D) Posture

Your body is loose and in balance. You are preparing yourself for an athletic feat. You are not, for example, standing as you would on a street corner waiting for the light to change.

From head to toes:

Head

Your head should align with your spine. Don't droop or sway.

Right Shoulder Lower

Since your right hand is lower on the shaft, the right shoulder dips a bit.

Arms Hang, Left Arm Straight

Arms should hang directly under the shoulders. The left arm is straight on a line with the clubshaft. The right elbow is a bit closer to the body than the left.

Bend and Flex

Bend from the hips, not the waist. Flex the knees just enough to find balance.

Weight Distribution

Weight is evenly distributed over both feet except when swinging the driver. On your drives, place a bit more weight (55-60 percent) on the right foot. Center

Looking Good
Patrick is ready to whale.
1) His head aligns with his spine.
2) His arms hang.
3) He's bent from the hips.
4) He's flexed at the knees.
5) He's loose, in balance and focused.

The club on the ground indicates the target line. Everything squares to it: eyes, shoulders, elbows, hips and feet. Just like he squared his clubface.

More Good Posture
6) His head is behind the ball.
7) His right shoulder is slightly lower.
8) His left arm is straight.
9) His feet are shoulder-width apart.
10) His left foot points out slightly.
11) His weight is evenly distributed.

Getting this right is a matter of practicing at home in front of a mirror.

The Ritual

Establish a procedure for setting up. It helps to organize your jumbled mind and puts you in a groove. First of all, determine the target line.

1

2

Next, determine your distance from the ball and square your clubface to the target line. Patrick seems to be utilizing the Whizzer's Stance although he would vehemently deny consciously doing so.

3

Establish your grip and square yourself away.

yourself over the middle of your feet. Not over toes or heels.

E) Now Line Everything Up
Square eyes, shoulders, elbows, hips and feet to the target line. Just like you squared your clubface.

Final Pointers
Ritualize the setup procedure for yourself:
1) Square the clubface to your target.
2) Establish your distance from the ball.
3) Square your stance and your body to the target line.
4) Establish your grip.
5) Make final adjustments and settle into a slot.

And once you're settled **forget about any more fidgeting and start your swing.**

4

5

Take one more look-see ... and fire away! It's important not to linger over the ball and think about each and every thing you're supposed to be doing. It'll only drive you nuts and make the ball smaller.

2 THE SWING BEGINS

This is news for most folks. Guys especially: Start out **slowly** *and keep your focus. Don't jerk the club up or back. Smooth and easy does it.*

A) The Takeaway

Left shoulder, left arm and clubshaft move away from the ball together. This is a smooth, one-piece movement that draws back low and straight along the target line for 18 inches or so. The takeaway is critical. Keep it square and gradual and your chances of meeting the ball flush on the downswing are very good. The takeaway is like the final countdown. You still have complete and conscious control of the swing. Make it good, because after this, you're on track, for better or worse.

B) The Backswing

The shoulders turn around a stable head and spine. Your head must act like the hub on a wheel. Left arm is still straight but not stiff. When the shaft is parallel to the ground, the toe of the clubhead must point straight up. If your grip and takeaway are right, this will happen automatically. At this point the clubshaft should be square to the target line.

As the backswing develops, more weight moves over the middle of your right foot. Your right knee should remain flexed throughout. Your head will move to the right, but don't fight it. Just make sure that it doesn't bob up and down.

C) The Top of the Backswing

At the top of the swing, the clubshaft should be horizontal to the ground and should point to the target. Your shoulders have turned 90 degrees and your hips

1   **2**

The Takeaway — You begin the swing with a smooth and steady, one-piece takeaway (club, hands and arms together). Draw back slow and straight.

1   **2**

The Backswing — When the club reaches this point (parallel to the turf) the clubhead should point straight up. This is a good checkpoint. Note Patrick's weight has begun to shift to his right leg.

At the Top — Note that Patrick's head has remained still throughout the sequence. His shoulders and upper body have rotated around it like a wheel around a hub. His club is parallel to the ground and points at the target.

Coiled and Ready for Release — The whole idea here is to wind it up nice and neat. The left shoulder has traveled underneath the chin and most of the weight is over the right leg. Knees are still flexed and ready to lead the charge.

45 degrees. Both hands are now above the right shoulder and your left wrist remains unbroken. At this point you are coiled to the max and ready for release.

Final Pointers

It's swing time. Your mind should be free of further speculation about your grip and setup.

Look at the back of the ball and focus on two things:

1) Drawing the club back smoothly and
2) S-BOB: Square Blade on Ball.

3 SWOOOSH!

Now you reap what you've sown. You can't make any meaningful adjustments at this point. Keep your eyes on the back of the ball and your head down.

A) Coming Back Down

Begin the downswing by turning your left knee and hip. Let your right elbow drop toward your right hip. Don't rush it. Acceleration should be smooth and gradual.

B) Downswing

Your body weight has shifted and is now evenly balanced over both feet. Arms are parallel to the ground and your hips swing square to the target line. Your shoulders follow, swinging slightly behind your hips.

C) Impact

Most of your weight is now over the left foot. Hips and shoulders have swung through the target line and your hands are directly over the ball. Your head remains down and behind the ball. Keep your eyes on the ball and think about hitting through it.

D) Follow-Through

Finish with your body weight over the outside of your left foot. The right foot is up on its toes. You should be perfectly balanced. Knees, shoulders and hips are level. Left toes, belly and right shoulder form a straight line.

Downswing — It begins by turning left knee and hip and letting the elbow drop. Patrick then pushes off his right side. His hips are moving ahead of his shoulders followed by arms, hands and club.

Impact — Weight has shifted to the left foot. Hips are turning through the target line followed closely by the shoulders. His hands are over the ball and his head remains down. The clubface is square to the ball and the target line. Patrick is thinking about driving through a wall.

Follow-Through — Finish with your body weight over the outside of your left foot. The right foot is up on its toes. You should be perfectly balanced. Knees, shoulders and hips are level. Left toes, belly button and right shoulder form a straight line.

Final Pointers

The lower body leads the upper body as you release from your coil and come back around. *Drive off the right side with your legs and lead with your hips.*

Think about meeting the ball square (S-BOB!) and swinging through it.

And That's All There Is To It (Oh, Pa-leese!)

There's too many things to remember!

The *Basic Swing* has lots of parts when it's dissected like this, and if you're not careful, it can really do a number on your head. It's wise to remember that everything mentioned here dovetails into one another. It's really meant to work and this is *the* way to hit a golf ball. It's not some sorry custom or ritual. If you keep at it, you will hit the ball and hit the ball well.

This game is too weird!

What's strange about golf is that it's so strange — from the grip, to the stance, to the posture, to the swing. There's absolutely nothing like it on earth and it all takes some getting used to. So take it slow and work on things one step at a time. The learning curve in golf is quite steep and time consuming. If you get impatient with it you'll literally go bonkers.

Just don't tell me to "put the fun in my funda-mentals!"

OK. Learning this stuff is not always *fun(!)*. There's some misery to wade through, my friends.

However, what's really great about the fundamentals is that although there's some flexibility and room for debate, by and large this is how ya do it. And when stuff goes haywire (and in this game it *always* does) you simply have to review the basic swing fundamentals to correct what's wrong.

As a rule, if your game goes bad, it's because you've developed some bad habit that runs contrary to the aforementioned basics. Or you're just forgetting something.

And once you get a *feel* for it, it's very cool. Because then you can devote yourself to playing and *hitting the target*. Not merely hitting. And that day *will* come.

CAN YOU MAKE IT ANY
EASIER?

Sure.

Set the ball up on a tee, choke up on the handle of
your club and use little baby half swings at first. This
will give you some control over the variables and allow
you to start making contact with the ball immediately.

Once you start knocking the ball around,
you'll gain some confidence and start having fun.
It's very important to start having fun
as soon as possible!

Whether you're choked up or not, the objectives are
always the same:

Strike the ball square (to the target line)
With the middle of the clubface (on the sweetspot)
Directly toward a target.

This realistically translates to:

Hit it up,
Hit it straight,
And hit it at something.

There you go.

Just So You Can Say You Hit the Doggone Thing

The Easy Way — Remember this? Start every shot by determining the proper distance from the ball. Note how Patrick has choked up on his club. The shorter length makes it easier to achieve contact.

Little Baby Swings — Patrick cuts back on his swing by at least half in order to gain as much control as possible.

5

6

Making Contact — Keep your eyes glued to the back of the ball and think about driving through it with a square clubface. Note that Patrick's follow-through is also cut short.

It's important to understand that despite the choking up and the half swings, all the elements of the Basic Swing are still utilized.

And that this is only a modification to be used temporarily in order to keep you cheerful (and to build confidence!) during those first few days on the range.

Teed Up — Placing the ball on a tee will make it easier yet.

YOU GOTS TO GET THE
FEELIN!

Golf is an endeavor that requires equally high levels of concentration and relaxation. You cannot hit the ball well without focus and you cannot hit the ball without a loose and easy swing. These two acts can be at odds. The key to joining them into a mutual force is rhythm.

Rhythm is the magical bridge between principal and action. It makes what we think about doing physically happen gracefully. Rhythm is the connection and the translator between mind, mechanics, club and ball.

A good friend of mine was having trouble with his swing a while back. He was an excellent golfer but as these things go he found himself in a rut where he was topping his drives. As he was entered in a longest drive contest at Pebble Beach (no less) he sought the help of a professional.

The pro watched him take a few swings and simply said, "Bobby Darin, 1962."

"Excuse me? What was that?" my friend asked.

"*Mack the Knife,*" he replied and he sang a snippet from the tune:

"*Oh, when that shark BITES!*
With his TEETH! dear ..."

The pro addressed a ball with his club and continued the musical lesson while he took a swing:

"Ba Ba BA! Ba
Ba Ba BA! Ba ..."

On the second *BA!* the pro hit a very sweet 250-yard drive down the middle of the fairway.

With Mack on his mind, my friend took a few more cuts and rediscovered the sweetspot for himself that day. He took his lounge act up to Monterey and beat his nearest competitor by ten yards.

The fundamentals are important. You gotta know them for sure. But a golfer must also learn to apply them with a sense of rhythm to make it really come together. Fundamentals all by themselves are merely mechanics. Like words without a melody.

So find a beat, set a tempo and let the swing sing.

He's Got It!!

1

 **2**

The Real Thing — Patrick puts it all together in this series of action photos. Although you can't see the club, you get a great feel for the actual body movement as well as the grace and form of a well executed swing.

3

 **4**

Check out His Parts! His head is the hub, his shoulders are the wheel and his legs and hips are the driving force that really swings the swing.

5

Whoooosh!!
There's nothing pansy about a carefully controlled 130 mile per hour golf swing. (Yep. That's how fast they can go.)

6

And Such a Pretty Finish
When you finally find yourself ending your swing this way, you're probably hitting it like a champ.

She's Got It!!

Form and Grace — Well enough of the guys already! Jaime Rae Sandoval shows why she's one of the top high-school golfers in San Diego County in this series of pix taken at Eastlake Country Club in Chula Vista, California.

Now <u>that</u> is a straight left arm!

The Lower Body Leads — Jaime Rae's hips swing through the target line first and pulls shoulders, arms and hands after them in a hurry. In pic #6, her club is almost a perfect extension of her left arm.

Simply Classic — You could drop a plumb line from Jaime Rae's right shoulder and it would fall exactly upon her left foot. This was an actual swing, folks. No posing.

A SUMMARY of Final Pointers

The Grip

The golf grip is a unique thing for a beginner to tackle. It's not just holding something. It affects the flight of every ball. **Explore the nuances for yourself carefully.** After all, it's your direct connection to the club and ball.

Grip gently with a touch of firmness. A tight grip will hamper feel, tense you up and blister your hands.

Setting Up

Ritualize the setup procedure for yourself:
1) Square the clubface to your target.
2) Establish your distance from the ball.
3) Square your stance and your body to the target line.
4) Establish your grip.
5) Make final adjustments and settle into a slot.

And once you're settled **forget about any more fidgeting and start your swing.**

The Swing Begins

It's swing time. Your mind should be free of further speculation about your grip and setup.

Look at the back of the ball and focus on two things:

1) Drawing the club back smoothly and
2) S-BOB: Square Blade on Ball.

Swoosh!

The lower body leads the upper body as you release from your coil and come back around. **Drive off the right side with your legs and lead with your hips.**

Think about meeting the ball square (S-BOB!) and swinging through it.

Rhythm

The fundamentals are important. You gotta know them for sure. But a golfer must also learn to apply them with a sense of rhythm to make it really come together. Fundamentals all by themselves are merely mechanics. Like words without a melody.

So find a beat, set a tempo and **let the swing sing.**

The Golf Course — The green is in the foreground
and the little fellow waaay in the back is standing at
the tee for this hole. In between is the fairway. There
are more than 23,000 courses in the United States
alone. It's one happening sport. Everybody plays!

Chapter Three

The Game

The Golf Course

Isn't it amazing that a game that requires so much real estate and so much maintenance is so popular? There certainly must be something to it.

A golf course is composed of either 18 different holes or nine different holes that are played twice in a regular game of golf. A hole is made up of a tee at the start (where play begins), a green at the end (where each golfer tries to sink their ball into the hole or cup) and a fairway in between.

The total of all the distances from each tee to each hole on an 18-hole regulation course usually measures between 6,000 and 7,000 yards, or about five miles. The entire area that comprises an 18-hole course is around 100 acres. Most 18-hole courses have four long holes measuring between 476 and 575 yards, four short holes measuring between 120 and 250 yards, and 10 medium length holes measuring between 251 and 475 yards.

Ideally, courses are designed to provide a suitable challenge for every golfer. Parallel holes are avoided and holes run in different directions so that wind may affect each hole differently. In addition, trees, bunkers, streams, ponds and ditches are scattered about to provide hazards and boundaries between holes.

Safety

Remember to keep a tree between you and anyone with a club in their mitts.

Golf balls can travel up to 100 miles an hour. When someone yells out FORE! it's time to duck and cover. Although it's only natural to try to spot the incoming missile, DON'T LOOK UP!

Be aware of all the action on your hole as well as on neighboring holes and stay well back of and behind your fellow golfer's swinging and shanking areas.

Make sure others are out of your range before hitting.

Health

Don't overdo it.

The swing can hurt your back. Especially if you're into driving hundreds of balls at the range. And if you own a jerky, violent swing, your chances of straining or tearing something is that much greater. Better to smooth it out, build up to it and pace yourself.

Etiquette

Golf is a peaceful, soft-spoken (HA!) game of concentrated effort played at a walker's clip. To be sure, anything that disturbs the peace is a breach of etiquette.

Don't move or talk when your opponent is playing his ball.

Don't heckle (smack, trash talk) your opponent unless he's a good friend and deserves it.

Don't stand too near or in his line when your opponent is playing the ball.

Don't loiter (slack, cruise, contemplate at length). Move it along.

If you lose your ball and it's taking a long time to find it, wave the players behind you to play through.

Obviously, it's a much better idea to simply put a time limit on such efforts in order to keep the game moving.

Repair any damage you may do. Replace your divots (hunks of turf lifted by your club), repair any pitch marks you've made on the green and rake out any footprints you've left in the bunkers (rakes are provided).

Scoring

Scoring is on the honor system. There are no referees. Each golfer is responsible for his own scoring. Cheating is VERY serious business in golf.

The object of the game is to hit the ball into the cup on each hole using as few strokes as possible. Scoring is done by counting all the strokes a golfer has accumulated over the course of play.

There are a number of scoring systems. The most popular and the most familiar method of play is called stroke play. Each golfer simply keeps track of his strokes and at the finish, the player with the fewest strokes wins. In stroke play, every hole must be completed by putting the ball into the hole.

In match play, players play against each other rather than the entire field. Each hole is scored separately and won with the lowest stroke count. The game proceeds until one player is more holes ahead than there are holes left to play. If after 18 holes the players are tied, or all square, they return to the first hole and play sudden death until one player wins a hole. In match

play, players don't always have to put their final putt
into the hole. The opponent may deem that the ball is
so close to the hole that it would be impossible to miss
and concede the putt.

There are other scoring systems. Rest assured that like
the ones described above, they reward only the lowest
stroke counts.

Handicapping

*Handicapping enables golfers of all standards to com-
pete with one another with an equal chance.*

Each hole on an 18-hole course is given a rating
depending upon its length. This rating is called par. Par
is the number of strokes a very good player in good
form would take to finish or hole out.

Most holes up to 250 yards in length are rated par 3.

Holes between 251 yards and 475 yards are usually
rated par 4.

Holes 476 yards and over are most often rated par 5.

If you take the aforementioned standard course of four
par-3 holes, four par-5 holes and 10 par-4 holes, the
total par for the course adds up to 72. Some courses
that are shorter in total length, called executive
courses, are rated lower. Others that are longer are
rated higher.

The par of the course acts as the yardstick by which a

player judges his performance and thereby gains his handicap. A player's handicap would be his average for the course minus the par for the course. Since a very good player would finish in an average of 72 strokes over a period of time, his handicap would be zero or scratch (72 minus 72 equals zero). The majority of players have handicaps from scratch to 24. The maximum for men is 24. The maximum for women is 36.

Thus, an 18-handicap player is one whose average score is 90 on a par-72 course (90 minus 72 equals 18).

In stroke play, the full handicap is deducted from the gross score. The player with the lowest net score is the winner.

In match play, a percentage of strokes is given by the lower handicap player to the higher handicap player. That percentage is 75 percent of the difference between the two handicaps. For example, if one player is a 6-handicap and the other is an 18-handicap, the difference is 12 and 75 percent of that is 9. So 9 strokes are given to the 18-handicap player. Where the strokes are taken is indicated by the scorecard for that particular course, which has a stroke index column next to each hole. A stroke is taken on each hole that has a handicap rating of 9 or less. If the difference results in a fraction, the number is rounded up to the nearest whole number.

Professionals are the only golfers without a handicap and are rated as scratch or 0.

Your First Games:
Laugh & Be Happy

What You Need

1) Basic Swing

I didn't play until I had hit about 1,650 balls over a span of about six months with about six weeks of very solid effort. I had professional lessons, *reliable* friendly lessons and studied lots of instructional material. Before I played a game, I could hit the ball with some authority (few misses, usually with some distance) and I hit the ball in the general direction of the flag (shots were not always straight, but they were manageable). In other words, I was capable of *moving the ball along* because I had the beginnings of a decent swing.

It's not so much that you should be a great hitter before you go out there, just a consistent one. And there's only one way to be such a player short of divine intervention.

You must have a working knowledge and a good feel for the *Basic Swing.*

2) Golf Clubs and Bag
Get a bag full of clubs. They don't have to be pretty. The following will do:
No. 3 Wood
No. 5 Wood
No. 4 through 9 Irons
Pitching Wedge
Putter

3) Three Golf Balls. Or
enough to back you up when you start losing them.

4) A Handful of Tees. And try to remember to pick
them up after you tee off.

5) An Enthusiastic Attitude. Be a happy hacker.
The alternative is pure misery!

6) Appropriate
Dress. Loose and comfortable. Remember, you're swinging. Inquire about dress codes.

7) Other Stuff

Footwear
Don't worry about spiked shoes for now. Your sneakers should work fine.

Protection from the Sun
You'll be out there for hours. Protect yourself.

Left-Hand Glove
A glove on your leading hand will prevent blisters when you're beginning and help your grip.

No Limits

Actually, your first games shouldn't even be games. They should be more like educational forays. No scoring, no penalties and no limits as to how many balls you hit. As long as you're not bothering anybody, do whatever it takes to really *play and learn* on a golf course. If you want to try another shot over again, *do it!* If you want to change your lie, *do it!* Experiment with the clubs and get to know what each one does. Be concerned about learning. Not about how many swings you're taking and what your darn score is. It's more carefree that way and more fun. This game is very, very challenging and will continue to be so. Keeping a scorecard and going by the book at this point will break your spirit.

Play with Others

The friendly pressure of others will help your concentration and you'll play your better. Other eyes can also lend advice and tell you things about your game. This is especially beneficial if your partners are more experienced than you. Golf is a social game and having others around is really a natural part of the sport. It gets rather lonely out there otherwise.

Play Nine Holes (or less) at a Time

Eighteen holes is a bit much for starters. It's like hitting 200 balls at the range instead of 50. Nine holes will give you more than a taste, and if it's a bad day for golfing it's that much shorter. Heck, nine holes will take you two hours anyway. That's quite enough!

Take a Deep Breath

The first time around is exciting and nerve racking. Even though you might be Joe Cool on the driving range, out on the fairways and especially the tees, your mind will detonate with a million useless thoughts or simply snap shut. You can't hit the ball when you're all keyed up, so relax. Or, as one of my mentors strongly suggests:

"Just Don't Give a Hoot!"

Laugh

When you miss. When you slice. When you hit a tree. When your putt rolls ten feet past the cup.

Sheriff John said it best:

"Laugh and be happy and the whole world smiles with you!"

Hokey but oh so true! If you can laugh at yourself and the game, you'll like yourself and the game a whole lot better. Your partners will love you for it, and the experience will take on a whole new dimension. Besides, who really cares if you're the world's greatest wannabee golfer anyway?

Loosen Up, You Knucklehead! And learn to laugh at your absolutely dismal performance. You *will* get better.

Meanwhile ... *Who Cares!!*

The Clubs — Basically you have woods and irons. The big blocky one is a wood and there are up to seven of those in various shaft lengths, clubhead sizes and clubface angles or lofts. The other two are irons. There are nine numbered irons, a pitching wedge and a sand wedge. The one in the middle is a 5-iron and the one in the back is a sand wedge. Note the different clubface angles and shaft lengths. The only other club type not pictured here is the putter.

Using Your Clubs

For those of you who still remember high-school shop (do they even have such a thing anymore?) it's time to remember the craftsman's motto:

"Always Use the Right Tool for the Job!"

In golf, choosing the right club for a particular shot is a very big deal. The reason there are 14 clubs in an official set of clubs is not to show off or just to throw at ducks.

You can say that clubs have as much to do with your game as your swing. Each club has a specific length and clubhead design built to hit a golf ball a specific way in specific situations for a specific distance *(see chart next page)*. It's important to know what each club does and even more important to discover what you can do with each.

The Clubs

Woods: No. 1 through 7

You don't use a screwdriver to hammer a nail, and you don't use a putter to move a golf ball 200 yards. You use what is called a wood to hit the ball for the greatest distances. Woods come in different sizes, and the new ones aren't made of wood anymore. Woods have the big clubheads and have the longest shafts of all the clubs. The heads are made of metal or wood. You use woods off the tee at the beginning of long holes, on the fairways and in certain lies in the rough when you need distance.

There are seven types of woods and they are numbered 1 to 7. The 1-wood has the biggest head, the longest shaft, the least amount of loft and hits the ball the farthest. The woods get progressively smaller, shorter, more angled and hit for less distance as they go up in number.

You use the *Basic Swing* to hit golf balls with the woods.

Long Irons: No. 1 through 3

The long irons are those irons numbered from 1 to 3. The 1-iron is seldom used any more and the 2-iron is too difficult for beginners to play. They have been replaced in many golf bags by the higher numbered/ lofted woods, which are much easier to hit. Among the irons, they have the longest shaft lengths and hit for the longest distances.

Approximate Yardage Per Club			
Club	Beginner	Average	Good
Driver	190	220	250
2-Wood	180	215	235
3-Wood	170	210	225
4-Wood	165	205	215
5-Wood	150	195	205
2-Iron	145	180	190
3-Iron	135	170	180
4-Iron	125	160	170
5-Iron	120	155	165
6-Iron	115	145	160
7-Iron	105	140	150
8-Iron	95	130	140
9-Iron	80	115	125
Wedge	70	100	110
Sand Wedge	55	80	95

This table gives you an idea of how clubs work. For example, you don't swing harder to make the ball go farther, you use the same swing with the appropriate club. By the way, these distances are only approximate. They are not intended to be a yardstick for ability. Everybody's different!

All irons have metal clubheads. Hence the name iron, though they are usually made from other types of metals these days. Like the woods, the loft gets loftier and the length gets shorter as you move up through the iron numbers. For example, the 1-iron has the least loft, has the greatest length and hits the ball farthest. The long irons are usually used to hit the ball for distance on the open fairways or off the tee.

Use the *Basic Swing* with the long irons.

Middle Irons: No. 4 through 6

Again, progressively shorter shafts and loftier blades yielding higher and shorter shots. Numbered from 4 to 6, the middle irons are useful in a variety of situations. These clubs are used for short tee shots, fairway shots, pitching, chipping, and even sand shots (shots from sand traps or bunkers).

Short Irons: No. 7 and Up

The irons numbered 7, 8 and 9, the pitching wedge and the sand wedge have the greatest lofts of all. The short irons are used for shots closer to the green, difficult shots from the rough, shots that require loft over obstacles and tee shots on very short holes. The short irons are generally used for pitching, chipping and sand shots.

Use the *Basic Swing* with both middle and short irons for some shots and variations thereof depending on the lie (where the ball is nestled) and the type of shot required.

MIDDLE & SHORT IRON SWING VARIATIONS

It's important to remember that the Basic Swing is the Mother of all Golf Swings. If you can't muster a Basic Swing, you can't do the variations, which are only slight variations at that.

Pitching

Say you're close to the green, but there's a sand trap or a shrub or a sleeping hobo in the way. The ball has to

Open Stance — In general, the stance is the same for both pitching and chipping. The left foot is drawn back a bit from a square position as indicated by the club lying on the turf. This enables the arms to make the shot without using legs and body.

Since you're close to the green, simple pitch and chip shots require shorter backswings than the full swings described previously.

Pitching and chipping are finesse shots since you're aiming at a more specific target area and gauging just how full your stroke should be. Through practice and experience, you'll learn which clubs do what with quarter and half swings.

go up and over, but not too far. You need an iron with lotsa loft, say a 9-iron or one of the wedges, with the following setup and swing:

From the basic stance, bring your left foot back a bit so that your stance is now open. This prevents your body and legs from getting too actively involved during the swing. Let your hands and arms play this shot. Use full, half or quarter swings depending on your distance from the hole. You will be able to judge the amount of backswing to use to cover various distances through practice and experience.

Except for the left foot position and the shorter swing arc (if need be), you're still executing the *Basic Swing*.

And by the way: let the club do the scooping for you. Don't try to scoop it up yourself. Just swing through the ball like you should always do, and let the tool do its thing.

Properly hit pitch shots will have backspin due to the steep angles of the loftier irons. This can prevent excessive rolling once the shot reaches the green.

Chipping

Now you're close to the green with no obstacles to fly over. Pick an iron with less loft, say a 6 or 7. Address and swing at the ball as you would a pitch shot. You will have more control of the ball because you don't have to worry about hitting it high, only straight. But since the ball will have less backspin, it will roll more than the pitch shot, so your backswing must be just so. Again, just how far back your backswing goes is a matter for you, the club and the course.

Sand Shots

Greenside Bunkers

The trick to hitting the ball out of a sand trap or bunker is to hit behind the ball. Using a specially designed club called the sand wedge, you play the ball off the left heel with the left foot pulled back like you played the pitch and chip shots.

With the blade turned slightly out or open, aim an inch or two behind the ball and let the deeply angled blade plow through the sand and throw the ball up and out of the bunker. It's important to hit all the way through and not let up. If the ball is buried, play the ball off the rear foot with the blade turned slightly in or closed. With practice, you'll get a feel for how far you draw the club back to achieve different distances. By the way, according to the rules, you are not allowed to ground your clubhead (set the blade of your club upon the sand) before you hit the ball.

Fairway Bunkers

This is a very difficult shot to hit for distance because it's hard to hit just ball and no sand. Address the ball so that it lies centered between your legs in order to hit the ball with a descending blow. Using an iron with enough loft to clear the lip of the bunker, square yourself to the target line and hit the ball cleanly.

The safer bet, of course, is to just get it out onto the fairway by using the method described previously for greenside bunker shots.

1

Blasting Out of the Pit

Again, note the open stance. You want to use only your arms to lift the ball up and out of the trap. Use an open blade, as shown, for most shots. When the ball is really buried, angle the blade in (closed).

2

Aim an inch or so behind the ball and lift both sand and ball.

3

Make sure you swing all the way through. Don't let the sand stop you in midstroke.

1

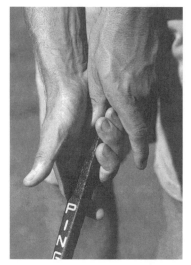

Reverse Overlap Grip for Putting

In order to get a better feel for the club with the right hand, the right hand closes completely around the shaft. The left thumb still snuggles into the palm of the right as before.

2

The left index finger wraps outside the right hand fingers.

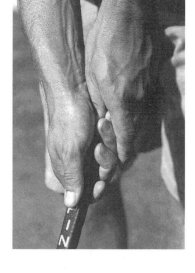

3

There you go.

PUTTING

When you're on the green, you tap the ball with a putter in order to roll the ball into the hole. Putters are designed in a variety of shapes and sizes and putting technique is almost all up to the whim of the individual golfer (within the rules of the game, of course). You read the roll and the cut of the green as best you can, line up your shot and tap that baby into the cup. It's a mental thing that requires practice, concentration and feel over any particular technique, although a million experts may tell you differently.

Eight Steps to Putting Glory

1) Use the reverse overlap grip. Hands are still knit together, however, the left index finger is placed over the right hand fingers in order to achieve a better feel for the swing.

2) Stance and posture is much the same as that of the *Basic Swing*. Feet, knees, hips and shoulders are square to the target line. The ball is lined up with the left heel. Your weight is evenly balanced over both feet and your knees are flexed. The head is kept still and positioned directly over the ball.

3) Aim for a much larger target than the hole. Try to place your putt within a three foot radius of the cup.

4) Pick your target line, then pick a spot one foot ahead of your ball on the target line and aim for that.

5) Swing from the shoulders. Wrists remain firm. Your club, hands, wrists and arms stroke in a smooth, one-piece motion. Like a pendulum do.

6) Hit the ball square and true to its target line.

7) Keep your head down throughout impact and follow-through.

8) The backswing equals the follow-through. If you draw back one foot, follow through one foot.

Other Stuff

Besides cultivating a positive attitude about putting, here are some specific tips you should know:

Uphill putts are easier to judge than downhill putts. Aim your shots to the green accordingly.

The speed of your putt is affected by wetness, the length of the grass and the grain of the grass's cut.

– Wet grass is slower than dry grass.
– Long grass is slower than short grass.
– Putting against the grain of the grass is slower than putting with it.

On sidehill putts, aim your putt slightly uphill to the cup.

Learn to judge the speed of your putts. Discover how hard you must hit your putts to achieve various speeds.

Your putter is more accurate than the other clubs. Always use your putter around the green if the grass isn't too high.

Par allows two putts per hole. That's 36 strokes. So practice your putts!

1

2

Putting — Find your target line and square yourself to it as you did with the Basic Swing. Place your head directly over the ball, aim for a spot about a foot in front of the ball, think a pleasant thought and draw back in a one-piece takeaway.

3

4

Like a Pendulum — Swing from the shoulders and hit your ball square. Follow through the exact distance that you swung back. Keep your head down until you hear the roar of the crowd.

1

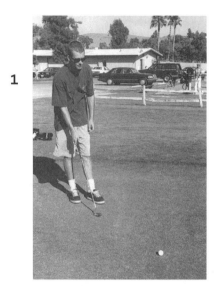

2

The Putting Ritual — Yes, another procedure. Patrick first determines his target line. Then he squares his putter and picks a point along the target to aim for. Again, this point is only a foot or so beyond the ball.

3

4

He establishes his grip, looks again at the hole and target line and settles into his putter's stance and posture.

Mr. Putter Squares Off — Putters come in all shapes and sizes. Largely because putting is perhaps the most whimsical part of the game. But what *really* counts is hitting the ball squarely to the target. Just like you do with every other club during each and every swing.

The Clubs: A Quick Rundown

Woods

1-Wood: Off the tee. Long and low.

3-Wood: Off the tee or long shots from poor fairway lies. Long and high.

5-Wood: Long shots from poor lies in the fairway or rough. Long and high.

6-Wood: More lofted than the 5-wood.

7-Wood: And even more loft. The 5- through 7-woods are used in place of the longer irons, which are much more difficult to use and not as effective in the rough.

Long Irons

1-Iron: Seldom used. Very difficult to use.

2-Iron: Off the tee or long shots from the fairway. Difficult to use. Being replaced by 5-woods.

3-Iron: Off the tee or long shots from the fairway. The longest iron most beginners can handle.

4-Iron: Off the tee on short holes or shots from fairway, rough or bad lies. Fairly long.

Medium Irons

5-Iron: Off the tee on short holes or shots from fairway or rough. May be used for pitch or pitch-and-run shots. Fairly high and long.

6-Iron: Shots from high grass or poor lies, clean lies in the sand, fairway, pitch-and-run or chip shots. Fairly high and long.

7-Iron: Shots close to green, chipping, pitching or sand shots. High loft and backspin.

Short Irons

8-Iron: Same as 7-iron. Greater loft.

9-Iron: Shots close to green, pitching or sand shots.

Pitching Wedge: Shots close to green, pitching or sand shots.

Sand Wedge: Sand shots or short pitches.

Putter: Strokes the ball on the green.

Special Situations

Bushes and Trees

If you can swing the club unimpeded through a clear path to the fairway give it a go. Otherwise reposition your ball and take the penalty according to the rules. If you choose to play the ball, use an iron with little loft, such as a No. 4 or 5-iron, in order to keep the ball low and to clear any branches or growth overhead. Grip down on the shaft to gain maximum control of your swing.

Wind

Crosswind

Aim off target into the wind and let the wind blow the ball back to your target line. This only works, however, if the winds are consistent and/or you hit it up there during a puff.

Into the Wind

Keep your shots low. Position the ball at the center of your stance so that your clubhead makes a descending blow to the ball.

With the Wind

Hit your ball high with an ascending blow by placing the ball forward toward your left toe.

Hills

Take something less than a full swing on these shots as it will be difficult to maintain your balance.

Uphill Shot, Right Foot Lower

To compensate for the incline, shift some weight to your left foot. The ball will fly to the left so adjust yourself to the target line accordingly.

Downhill Shot, Left Foot Lower

Position the ball toward the middle of your stance to make a descending blow. Flex your knees in order to better reach the ball. Compensate for a ball that flies to the right.

Sidehill Shot, Below the Feet

Center the ball and flex your knees to reach the ball properly. Allow for a shot that flies right.

Sidehill Shot, Above the Feet

Center the ball and allow for a shot that flies left.

Uphill Shot, Right Foot Lower — To compensate for the incline, shift some weight to your left foot. Ball flies left.

Downhill Shot, Left Foot Lower — Center the ball, flex the knees and make a descending blow. Ball flies right.

Sidehill Shot, Below the Feet — Center the ball and flex the knees. Ball flies right.

Sidehill Shot, Above the Feet — Center the ball, choke up, if need be, and flex the knees. Ball flies left.

89

Special Situations

Chapter Seven

(Some)
Rules

Here are some rules that apply to situations you'll probably encounter with some frequency or need to make note of before too long.

The *United States Golf Association (USGA)* determines the rules of golf in the United States. The complete book of rules is called the *Rules of Golf* and your pro shop will probably have it. If they don't, call or write:

USGA
Order Department
Liberty Corner Road
PO Box 708
Far Hills, NJ 07931
800-336-4446

Again, these are only <u>some</u> of the rules.

○ Play only the American-size golf ball.

○ You can use up to 14 clubs.

○ Tee up between the tee markers and up to two club lengths behind them.

○ The player who won the last hole plays first from the next tee. Or play *ready golf.* See below.

○ The player whose ball is farthest from the hole plays first. Or, to speed up play for casual rounds, golfers play *ready golf:* whoever is ready plays.

○ You must hit the ball with your clubhead. You cannot push or scrape the ball.

○ Play the ball where it lies except in special situations noted in the course rules.

○ You may replace a damaged ball without penalty.

○ Play the course as you find it.

○ You are not allowed to move, bend or break anything fixed or growing when making your swing. You cannot press down on the turf behind the ball or prepare the area around your ball in any way.

○ You cannot ground your club (touch the ground with your club) in a hazard. A hazard is a bunker (sand or grass trap) or water.

○ If your ball hits the wrong green, you may drop it off without penalty.

○ You may remove stones and leaves except in hazards.

○ If an obstruction is made by man, you may move it without penalty. If it is unmovable, you may drop your ball two club-lengths away without penalty, but not nearer the hole.

○ If you move your ball, you play it where it drops and add a penalty stroke.

○ If someone or something else moves it, you play it where it lies without penalty.

○ If you lose your ball or hit it out of bounds, you must replay the stroke and add a penalty stroke.

○ If your ball is unplayable, you may treat it like a lost ball, or you may drop the ball at least two club-lengths, not nearer the hole, behind the unplayable spot and add one penalty stroke. If you're in a bunker, you must re-drop it in a bunker.

○ If your ball goes in a water hazard, you may drop the ball behind the hazard or where you last played and add one penalty stroke.

○ If your ball lands in casual water (water that appears from a patch of turf when you step on it), or in an area

marked Ground Under Repair, or in an animal's bur-
rowing hole, you may drop the ball as near as possible
to the original lie, but not nearer the hole. On the
green or in a hazard, you may drop the ball within two
club-lengths of the original lie, not nearer the hole.

○ Dropping the ball is done by facing the hole and
dropping the ball at arms length from a standing position.

○ If the ball lands nearer the hole, more than two club-
lengths away, goes into a hazard or strikes you before it
hits the ground, you must redrop your ball.

○ Drops in a hazard must remain in the hazard.

○ If another ball is in your path on the green, you may
have it marked and lifted.

Chapter Eight

2,000 Swings,Five Games & A Slice

A Beginner's Journal

This journal covers a span of 30 years although I didn't get serious until the last year. I had a glimpse of golf as a kid, a taste when I was in my 30s, a large chunk almost 10 years later and, finally, during one Summer, I became a serious poser.

The original journal included an accounting of my every swing. Don't worry, I didn't print the whole thing here because it would be much too boring. For example, I deleted entries such as:

June 7: *Today I hit 50 balls with a 5-iron. I sliced 40 balls, topped eight and missed one completely. I hit one straight, but I don't know why.*

What I kept had to be what I considered at least somewhat entertaining and/or informative.

Keeping a journal is a great tool to include in your learning process. It makes you *think* about what you're doing, and it will give you *perspective* on your efforts over time. Don't take just my word on that, either. One of the game's true giants, Ben Hogan, kept a journal of his practice sessions, and it helped him to develop one of the most legendary swings in golf history.

Anyway, here it is — the tale of a beginning golfer. May your road be less bumpy, but just as much fun.

Part One: First Tastes

A Very Long Time Ago: Feelin' Bad for Dad

My first experiences with golf came at the age of 11 or so when I caddied for my Dad. I have only one vague memory of that and it's vague for good reason. My Dad was a remarkably talented man in many, many ways, but, like so many of us, he was a lousy golfer.

> *In fact, his whole head starts to turn red and I'm thinking that something's gonna blow. And, no kidding, his nickname is Red.*

In this memory I'm squatting in a bushy rough at the Mapledale Country Club in Dover, Delaware. I'm watching Dad hack away at a ball nestled somewhere in the knee-high grass. I'm quietly and desperately rooting for him to hit the ball, but he just keeps swinging and missing. With every horrendous stroke, I watch his face get redder and redder from the effort and frustration. In fact, his whole head starts to turn red and I'm thinking that something's gonna blow. And, no kidding, his nickname is Red.

Of course, like most young boys who love their Dads, this made me feel pretty awful. In fact, I probably felt worse than he did. The old *son-sees-father-as-less-than-conquering-hero* type of thing. I'm certain that Dad finally did hit the darn ball that day and probably even played a decent game for a guy who didn't play much (or even cared to), but it's the swinging and missing and his big red face that I remember. Now, I wouldn't entirely blame that memory for not trying the sport at an earlier age, but I'm sure it was influential.

Actually, I was more put off by the somewhat elitist image that golf and golfers seemed to project during that period. Golf was definitely upper crust (or at least upper middle class) stuff at one time, and not a common man's game at all. Today you see the entire spectrum of humanity swatting balls, but not so long ago, it was mainly middle aged white guys in uniform (white belts, white shoes and polyester was the stereotype) posturing like so many preppie wannabees. When I was growing up, they and their ilk were quite literally the enemy of most young people in America. If golf was *their* game it certainly was not mine. Finally, there was no indication that golf was really any fun at all. I didn't get it. Where was the action and the thrill? It appeared to me to be just one more suburban ritual. Like going to work five days a week and attending church on Sunday. Bo-ring!

So for many years I never went near a golf course. I didn't even think about it. The game of golf was as foreign to me as cricket.

Look Out! I Mean, FORE!
I didn't even swing a club until I was 34.

A friend who had become a recent convert suggested I give the game a try. He gave me a call one night and invited me to join him and his wife at the driving range. "Golfing is fun! And I betcha you'll be great at it!" he exclaimed.

As it turned out, I was much less than great, but I did hit a golf ball over 200 yards that night.

It was the very first ball from the bucket. It went straight and true, and I never felt it leave the driver. It just *projected* from the tee to the far end of the range. My friend was delightfully surprised and said I must be a *natural*. For a brief period I believed him. After all, it was such a simple thing to do.

> *It rocketed straight for a row of golfers to my right and my heart stopped. Everyone scattered and some even hit the ground flat.*

But I hit the turf in *front* of the ball on my next swing and it *really* rattled my bones. I missed the ball *and* the turf on my third swing, and I nearly flipped over because I was swinging so doggone hard. In my final attempt, I nicked the ball in such a way that it flew off to the side, *a full 90 degrees* from the direction I intended. It rocketed straight for a row of golfers to my right and my heart stopped. Everyone scattered and some even hit the ground flat.

Lucky for me no one got hit. Twenty unfriendly faces turned and stared. To this day I have never heard of a ball doing that, but, I swear, it happened just that way.

I was so shaken and embarrassed that I put the driver down and turned the remaining 98 balls in. It was almost 11 years before I took up golfing again.

> *There are a million ways to do the simplest thing in golf and there are a thousand other things to remember while you're trying to do it.*

Part Two: Really Trying
Repeat After Me!

When I finally expressed interest in playing again, a good friend loaned me some ancient clubs that his uncle had given him, and I signed up for some lessons at the local public golf course. The clubs were wood shafted with their leather grips starting to unravel. Nobody could tell me how old they were, but everyone agreed that they belonged in a museum. My instructor thought they were pretty cool, though, and said that if I could learn to play with them, I could hit the ball with anything. Obviously, I didn't know from Adam, but I knew I wasn't going to buy a new set of clubs until I knew I could hit the ball, and hit the ball in the right direction, with the borrowed clubs.

I went to the range with my friend to try them out, and I did all right. I hit some and botched many more, but none flew sideways this time, and I even found the sweetspot on a couple. It definitely felt good enough to carry on, although I blistered one of my hands from gripping too tightly.

I signed up for five lessons for $100 with a real cool guy who used to be an explosives expert in the Navy. Seems one day he realized that all he really wanted to do was play golf, so he made a midlife left turn and got into the game as an instructor with aspirations to play professionally.

Despite the correctness of the technique, it felt so stupid having a hand gripping my skull that I just couldn't concentrate.

Actually, before I even started swinging, I went to the library and checked out a bunch of how-to golf books. I read through about three or four and got an idea of what to expect. It helped, but I also got a taste of the information and conceptual overload that pervades this sport. There are a million ways to do the simplest thing in golf, and there are a thousand other things to remember while you're trying to do it. Everybody has an opinion and everyone has written a book about it. It has to be the most discussed and dissected subject on earth. Right up there with sex, politics and religion.

The lessons were good because of the instructor, but worrisome because of all the information. We worked on the stance and swing the whole time. I used my old clubs, but he let me use a more modern one once in a while and the difference was profound. The older clubs have a very small sweetspot so I had to hit the ball just right to make it sail. All the newer clubheads have expanded sweetspots that are more forgiving, as they say, with metal or graphite shafts that are lighter and easier to swing. Of course, if you're still swinging like a lumberjack, it doesn't matter if the sweetspot is the size of a dime or as wide as a manhole cover.

During the lessons, I never hit with woods, only irons. Actually, only the 5-iron. I was just trying to *hit* the ball. Grip, stance and swing all in sync. I learned that the 5-iron is pretty much the middle iron in a bag of golf clubs. The smaller numbered irons have less of an angle in their heads, which makes it harder to hit the ball. Those are used for distance. The irons numbered above 5 have increasingly greater angles, which make it easier to hit the ball. The greater angle gives the ball loft and less distance. Drivers, with their big blocky heads and long shafts, have huge sweetspots to send the ball the farthest of all.

I can imagine a sort of golfer's graveyard where they take all the short-circuited beginners, spray them with a coat of plaster and sell them as lawn ornaments.

I practiced in between the weekly lessons and found that I tired quickly. Mentally, that is. I'd usually hit a couple of balls well at first, but then the ball would start to shrink. I'd become befuddled and everything would go straight to hell. So, in the beginning, I'd buy only the warm-up basket of about 20 balls. That's all I could handle.

The one thing I really hated about the lessons was the way my instructor held my head (in order to keep it still) when I swung. Despite the correctness of the technique, it felt so stupid having a hand gripping my skull that I couldn't concentrate. I also kept thinking that I was going to hit him during the swing, although I never did. He had alotta little tricks like that. One thing about golf instruction: there is an endless stream of hints, tips and rules that is absolutely overwhelming.

Sometimes I would simply freeze when I addressed the ball. I'd set up, think about everything I was supposed to do, and go completely numb. I can imagine a sort of golfer's graveyard where they take all the short-circuited beginners, spray them with a coat of plaster and sell them as lawn ornaments.

I finally got to the point where I'd hit one good ball for every 10. But it was still pretty streaky. Sometimes I'd hit three good shots in a row and then I couldn't hit beans. Sometimes I'd hit one solidly and then whack 15 toppers in a row. I tried to keep my expectations low. I really only wanted to hit the ball. If I missed the ball completely only once or twice during a session, I was happy. I stubbornly kept using my borrowed clubs although the grip unwound on my 5-iron, so I used the 6-iron, which also unwound, so I used the 7-iron.

After two or three lessons my instructor had me hit the ball with something called the Medicus, which is a medieval device held together with hinges. You can only swing it successfully with a Perfect Swing. Otherwise it will flop on its hinges and prevent you from striking the ball. The theory is that you either learn to swing it right or go mad with frustration trying. As ridiculous as this sounds, the Medicus is one of those gizmos that really turn golfers on. But then any golfing gizmo turns golfers on. Seems this sport thrives on widgets guaranteed to *improve your game*. Gizmos are to golfers as health and beauty aids are to unhealthy and unattractive people (*maybe, just maybe this will work!*). I did hit a few with the Medicus, but only because the gods smiled. And in all fairness to the Medicus, it certainly is an impressively engineered contraption. Maybe they could do something with snowboards or tennis rackets.

After four weeks I got to the point where I had some good outings. I actually hit one ball well for every five hit poorly. I'd practice with my clubs, the instructor's 5-iron and even the Medicus. I began to think I was making progress. I was on my way!

The fifth and final lesson, however, was a disaster. I hit the ball worse than I had a month earlier. When he put his hand on my head to keep it from bobbing, I snapped. Throwing the club down I said, "I quit. This friggin game is for the birds."

Gizmos are to golfers as health and beauty aids are to unhealthy and unattractive people (maybe, just maybe this will work!).

I was about to storm off, when he squared himself in front of me like a drill instructor (or a former explosives expert) and barked, "Look at me!"

"What?" I asked, taken aback by his sudden assertiveness.
"I said LOOK AT ME!" He made a fork with his fingers and pointed

> *An announcer went up to him after he'd finished a round to get the usual mindless patter, but got a rousing and refreshingly candid, "I can't hit sh-t today!" from the pro instead.*

it at my eyes and then to his in no-nonsense punching motions.

So I looked at him.

"Repeat after me!"

"What?"

"I said REPEAT AFTER ME! I - can - hit - the - ball!"

"Uh, I can hit the ball?"

"AHH CAINT HEAR YOOO!"

"I - CAN - HIT - THE - BALL!"

I started to laugh, of course, and apologized. It wasn't his fault I was such a spaz.

He smiled and said, "Don't apologize. It's OK. I wondered when it was going to happen."

"What's that?"

"I wondered when you'd blow."

"Yeah, but ... I shouldn't have ..."

"But everybody does. Welcome to golf. You have arrived."

He then proceeded to tell me about all the times he'd tossed his clubs, broken his clubs and sent entire bags into the drink. "It got expensive so I stopped doing that. Much better to shrug it off and laugh. It's just a game."

Then he told me about some big name pro who used the S word the week before on national television. Apparently, an announcer went up to him after he'd finished a round to get the usual mindless patter, but got a rousing and refreshingly candid, "I can't hit sh-t today!" from the pro instead. Such frankness is frowned upon at that level, and the pro was fined quite a lot of money.

I felt better after hearing those tales and tried to hit a few more, but it was hopeless. So we laughed and shook hands and thus went my golf graduation day. I had joined the ranks of the hapless and confused and decided to try not to give a hoot. I knew deep down that the latter would be no small challenge.

Watching Strugglers

By the way, I had yet to play a game of golf. I was determined to master my swing and hitting ability before I ventured out on a course. There was no way that I was going to take my half-baked swing out on the fairway and suffer like so many others do.

During one lesson, we were swinging on a part of the range next to the first hole. Two guys were teeing off, and I decided to watch. They looked the part: nice pants, good equipment, snappy shoes. I figured that they must be good. Maybe I'd learn something.

Shouldn't those guys be arrested or something? Playing that poorly can't be legal! And to think that they were going to go through all that seventeen more times!

But it was ugly. Those two fellas dribbled off the tee, dribbled their shots up the fairway, and after a dozen botched shots, finally got to the green where they scored in double digits. I was stunned. Where was the Golf Patrol? Shouldn't those guys be arrested or something? Playing that poorly can't be legal! And to think that they were going to go through all that *seventeen more times!*

It made me feel better to see them struggle, but at the same time, it set my resolve to learn to hit consistently before teeing up. It's one thing to swing and miss on the range, but to do it on the course in front of God and everybody else is another. I knew that

> *A black hole forms in my mind each time I address the little white ball.*

doing that would send me into a fit from which I might never recover. I vowed I would stay on the range until I could indeed hit the ball *every single time.*

Part III: Charging Hard

5-26: Committed

After almost a six-month layoff due to a special project that came up, I decided to step up to the plate.

I packed away the old, beat-up clubs and spent an afternoon shopping for new ones. I thought about buying used stuff, but after checking out the retreads in various places, the lure of shiny newness proved too strong. First, I hefted the most expensive club I could find and then the cheapest. To my relief I discovered that I couldn't tell the difference. There was still a lot to choose from, though, and I almost got one of those museum headaches I get whenever I see too much in too short a time. Of course, I got advice from sales people and customers, I hit balls in indoor ranges, and I even got brief lessons a time or two, but after three stores, nothing jumped out at me. At last, just before I hit overload, I found the equipment that looked about right, felt about right and was priced about right. I got everything I needed (woods, irons, putter, bag and glove) for $300. And that ain't bad. Just *one* brand name club can cost that much.

Watch out world.

6-13: A Black Hole

A black hole forms in my mind each time I address the little white ball. I'm talking about that moment just before the takeaway. I've settled into my stance and my grip. I've aligned myself and the clubface to my target. I've loosened my limbs, adjusted my hands, my head and whatever for the very last time and all that's left is eye contact with the ball. That's precisely when normal time is suspended and a sort of dream state takes over.

Sometimes at this point, I feel confident and sometimes I feel muddled. If I feel too weird I back off and readdress the ball. That's also when my mind plays tricks, goes into overdrive or simply freezes. I'm not a Zen Master so I can't really define the phenomenon any better than that, but I know that *that tiny point of time* holds an important key to hitting the ball on the button.

6-16: Even My Wife Is Laughing at Me!

I went to the library and checked out eight books about golf instruction. I was particularly concerned about my grip, which I seem to adjust constantly, and which I feel is responsible for the slice (a ball that spins wildly off to the right) I've developed. One book in particular by Sam Snead was easy to read and understand. I practiced his recommended grip with a club at home, then my wife, Kathleen, and I headed out to the driving range. Using the 5-iron, I hit the first four balls on the money. "Wo-ho Doug!" she said with admiration.

I swung and missed completely the next two balls.

"You did that on purpose!" she laughed.

I said, "No, I was really trying. See what I mean about this damn game?" She laughed harder.

I regrouped, hit exactly 23 (a few on the button) and missed two more times. All in all, not a bad session at this point, but

*"You were sticking your butt out and flying at the elbows, too,"
she added.*

I'm slightly perturbed that I swung and missed four balls in front of Kathleen. Searching for more encouragement, I asked her what she thought of my form. I'm sure that even when I missed those four balls I probably looked pretty good at least.

Again, she laughed. "You want me to tell you?"
"Well, yeah."

"After you missed that first ball you started spreading your legs farther and farther apart before you swung."

> *Here's the thing: The ball is just sitting there. The only action in the game is what you bring to it. Just before you begin your swing, there's a great stillness in the world that the mind simply cannot tolerate.*

"Really?"

"It looked like you were about to do the splits or something. What was that all about?" More chuckles.

This is a surprise at first, but then I see it. When I missed the ball, I began making all sorts of conscious and unconscious adjustments. I thought I was just moving my hands but apparently I was wriggling all over the place.

"You were sticking your butt out and flying at the elbows, too," she added.

Oh, man! *This* I've got to work on. I thought about it for a bit as we walked back to the car, and I began to realize what was going on. Every time I missed a shot, I'd lose my focus and rhythm. I'd start thinking about stuff and just hang over the ball too long. I thought of a snippet from a song I couldn't quite place and rewrote the words in my mind:

Imagination sets in
Purty soon I'm swingin
DOINK DOINK DOINK
There goes a muffed shot

Next time I'm gonna set up and swing promptly each time, no matter what. I'm gonna let my body take over and put my mind on hold, where it can do less damage. Maybe I'll take a break or two, but I will not hover over the ball and let my brain explode all over my swing.

Here's the thing: *The ball is just sitting there.* The only action in the game is what you bring to it. Just before you begin your swing, there's a great stillness in the world that the mind simply cannot tolerate. There's no wind or wave to ride, no speeding ball to hit or catch, no gravitational forces hurtling you down a snowy slope. In an action sport, players must react to something and react quickly. You play or perform with instinct. *You don't think, you act!*

In the absence of anything to react to, the mind makes up stuff to fill the void and screw you up:

Watch out! Your grip is wrong! You're too close to the ball! Make an adjustment NOW! And make another DURING YOUR SWING! Your swing's too flat! Your arm's not straight! Keep your head still! And so on ...

It's like having a monkey on your back. Much better to do your thinking *before* you stand over the ball. Let your training, no matter how little, take over at that point. *In other words, just swing!*

6-16: A Pair of Real Swingers

There are these two guys I always see at the range. They always set up next to each other and hit like a thousand balls each. They have a camcorder to record their countless swings, and every few minutes, they carefully fiddle with it in order to get it just so.

In fact, everything they do is *just so*. They don't ever just swing away. Every ball is placed and targeted with care. Each guy fusses over his ball like it's to be the shot of shots. They align themselves with clubs on the ground. They step behind the ball, hold out their irons and squint at their target. They step up

Much better to do your thinking before you stand over the ball. Let your training, no matter how little, take over at that point. In other words, just swing!

> *Exclusive country clubs will remain as fashionable as money until doomsday, but the advent of public golf courses has opened the game to Everyman and Everywomen USA.*

to the ball and set up. They step back and make their practice cuts. They break down each part of their practice cut by stopping in various places and gazing at arms, hands, feet and legs. They readdress the ball and settle into their postures. They slowly take their clubs back and with silky smooth swings crush the ball into sharp trajectories. The impact is always quiet. Just a crisp click! and away they go every single time.

They pace themselves like a finely tuned artillery unit. Every move is connected, coordinated and precise. Although their concentration level must be off the scale, their demeanor is poised and relaxed. Almost lazy looking. But this is deceiving because even with all their posturing, they pound out shots twice as fast as the more frenzied hackers surrounding them. If I watch for too long, I become mesmerized. Their performance is so absorbing that I forget about my own practice and simply gawk. Wadda show!

When I resume my routine, I wonder if they ever notice me. I make so much more noise than they do! For example, my shots never click! off the club. They make a loud whacking noise because I'm always missing the sweetspot. I also grunt when I swing and curse when the ball goes every which way. Maybe when I'm not looking, they're filming me for laughs. Heck, I would.

I used to feel uncomfortable around them, but I'm not embarrassed anymore. I really admire their swings, and I like to be around such graceful expertise. It might rub off. Besides, these guys, like everyone else out there, are so absorbed in their own game that you'd have to show up buck naked and doused in pink paint before you'd be noticed. Like they say, golf is a game you play within yourself.

Every (wo)man's Game

There are now 26.2 million golfers in the United States at more than 16,057 golf facilities who spend $24.3 billion in green fees and golf equipment each year.*

Ahh, numbers! Big, BIG numbers that tell us that golf is indeed one of the Great American Games, and not simply the pursuit of the well-to-do as it once was. Of course, this is hardly news to anyone who has visited a golf course in recent years. Sure the plaid and multicolored peacocks of *Caddyshack* fame can still be spotted scooting about in their custom go-carts, and exclusive country clubs will remain as fashionable as money until doomsday, but the advent of public golf courses has opened the game to Everyman and Everywomen USA.

Take a drive by the fairways and you'll see shorts, T-shirts, jeans and baseball hats on folks of every shape, size and color. The vast middle class has taken to the links like they hunt, fish, bowl, shoot hoops and play softball. Yeah, you can still make it an outdoor business meeting, or a symbol of status or a fashion ritual if you'd like, but, underneath all the pomp and circumstance, golfing's real appeal is based on two things:

> *Underneath all the pomp and circumstance, golfing's real appeal is based on two things:*
>
> *1) It's fun and, therefore, a pretty cool thing to do*
>
> *2) And because it's so fun, it's highly addictive.*

1) It's fun and, therefore, a pretty cool thing to do
2) And because it's so fun, it's highly addictive.

*www.golfchannelsolutions.com/markets/usa

> *I'm hoping that all this exposure will sort of seep into the pores of my sub-conscious, arrange itself properly in my psyche and transmit all the proper signals to all my body parts without me really knowing it.*
>
> *Fat chance!*

6-17: Always Hope

Today I went out twice with the beginning of an agenda. Using a 5-iron, I kept the sessions short. I hit about 30 balls each time. I didn't want to get stale or bored.

Still stinging from my wife's observation about my splitting stance, I took practice cuts with my feet close together. This gave me a good feel for balance. If I can swing comfortably with my feet side by side, I certainly should have the confidence to swing with my feet in a more normal position.

I also quickened the pace of my shots. If I don't linger, my mind won't have the time to wander and second guess. I had some success, but I hit the ball with a pronounced slice. The clubhead is not meeting the ball square.

During the afternoon session, the folks around me were hitting about as bad as me. Either I'm getting better or Mondays must be Lousy Golfer's Day.

I witnessed what must have been a very young man's first lesson with Pop. "I can't hit the ball, Dad!" he wailed after a swing and a miss. I couldn't hear the father's quiet response, but his tone was patient. The kid was all arms and legs like a little deer trying to walk for the first time. He tried another wobbly swing and, by golly, he hit the ball! This tiny miracle inspired me because despite the lad's utter lack of form he made contact.

There is hope for us all!

6-18: May It All Sink In!

Although my actual practice sessions are short, at home I grip and swing the club a bit and do a lot of reading. I checked out eight how-to golf books from the library over the weekend and dug into a number of golf mags I had bought earlier in the month. The mags have tips on everything.

The danger, of course, is info overload. The trick is to know what you want to work on and seek info on just that. Then I filter it a bit and ease it into actual practice. I'm beginning to see the connections in my mind as well as in my experiences. Although the information available is mountainous and each writer has his particular slant, the fundamentals seem to be fairly consistent. At least, in a general way, stuff is dovetailing.

I'm hoping that all this exposure will sort of seep into the pores of my subconscious, arrange itself properly in my psyche and transmit all the proper signals to all my body parts *without me really knowing it.*

Fat chance!

I've gotten to the point that if I hit a few on the button, nobody gets hurt and folks are friendly, it's a good day. Even if I top 55 balls.

6-19: This Is a Good Day?

Not a great session today despite going back for baskets of balls. I ended up hitting about 100 balls (didn't I say I wouldn't do that anymore?) with a 4-iron. The slice was there but not on every shot. Topped the ball mostly. Hit a few nice, straight shots but not consistently. It's more difficult to hit with the 4-iron. The loftier clubs are more forgiving. I worked on square takeaways and bringing the club all the way back. I think I've been laying off a bit (not bringing the club all the way back) and that may be contributing to Mr. Slice. It's still a wonder why some balls sail and others dribble. Oh well.

> *He had a screwed-down hairdo with a bristly looking pony tail sticking straight out from the top of his head. The overall effect of his size, looks and violent play was pretty awesome. Like a warrior-dance or something.*

Met with a young friend who said I should start playing games. He said, "I was afraid to play at first, too. But when I got out there I didn't want to embarrass myself so I concentrated. I did better than I thought I would."

We'll see. I am anxious to proceed with this golfing stuff. I mean, what the heck.

I did manage to hit a divot near some guy's backside who was hitting next to me. I didn't say anything and neither did he. I just moved over a space. Then I sliced one over the partition, which has got to be 80 feet high, and narrowly missed two guys on the ninth hole. I looked the other way.

I've gotten to the point that if I hit a few on the button, nobody gets hurt and folks are friendly, it's a good day. Even if I top 55 balls.

6-20: Golfers

Some interesting asides:

A group of Samoan men were hitting next to me. One guy was terrific and hit these whopping shots with the mellowest swing. He'd hit a few then go over to chew with the boys who were gathered behind him on a nearby bench. Most of them took turns practicing this way. Slow and easy with lots of jaw breaks.

One of them, however, didn't take breaks. He wasn't very good. Maybe even worse than I. He was flaying with a wood and the balls were just screaming off the tee in all directions: *Thwack! Thwack! Thwack!* He was a big boy and the *Whooshing!* sound that his club made was particularly fearsome.

He had a screwed-down hairdo with a bristly looking pony tail sticking straight out from the top of his head. The overall effect of his size, looks and violent play was pretty awesome. Like a warrior-dance or something. All he needed was war paint, and I'm sure he would have had the range and the course all to himself. In fact, the guy wasn't supposed to be hitting with a wood where he was. But the range manager, who saw him clearly enough, was not about to tell *him* that.

On the other side of me were a couple of fat guys with beers who were also hacking away with woods. The range manager had no problem instructing those guys to cool it with the heavy clubs. They cheerfully obeyed and continued their debacle with irons for a few strokes but decided to leave soon thereafter. Like the slobs they were, they left beer cans, empty ball baskets and about 15 balls scattered over two tee areas. Well, lucky me. I hit their discarded balls when my balls were gone, cleaned up their beer cans and thought about calling it quits.

All my discoveries and minor victories concerning my initial swinging and hitting all come back to the fundamentals.

I always want to hit my last one good, though, and as a rule my last shots are usually bad. I get tired or something and everything starts to shake loose. Anyway, I spotted a ball stuck in the fence that guarded us from the other side of the range, plucked it out and gave it a chop. It went up at least but made a huge honking midair slice. Good night.

6-21: So That's It!

All my discoveries and minor victories concerning my initial swinging and hitting all come back to the fundamentals. It's like: I read or am told the basics, but nothing sinks in until I begin hitting the ball well and analyze why. *Oh, my slice is better because I'm drawing the club back straighter. Yeah, that's it. Keep everything square to the target.*

Of course, I was told all of that months ago, but doing it and having it come together at last is like learning it for the first time. It feels like I've discovered something new but in reality it has just taken a long time for my brains and nerve endings to get a clue.

6-27: Improvement!
A disciplined and productive session (for a change!).

I concentrated on specific parts of my swing.

Too many times my swings have been unfocused. They've been Hail Mary-type things without a real focused effort that in turn yields a feeling that the swing is on track and the ball will be hit cleanly.

1) *Stance:* I used a stance a bit wider than I had been using. A good shoulder-width apart. This feels better, more stable, of course, than the narrower ones I had been using.

2) *Left foot turned out in stance:* This also felt good. I'd been squaring my feet to the target line. This seems to help reduce my slice in particular.

3) *Distance from ball:* I calculated this carefully. I'm sure this is critical in order to hit the ball flush.

4) *Knees flexed:* This also affected my distance from the ball. When I'm not in the crouch, I miss-hit.

5) *Grip:* I placed my left hand a tad farther over to the left today. So that my left thumb was more naturally cupped in my right hand when it folded over. I also tried bringing my right thumb and forefinger closer together. Grip advice from Ben Hogan's *Five Lessons*.

6) I also concentrated on *square and steady takeaways*. My eye *focused on the ball*.

All my shots are straighter. Even the toppers. Some very good shots. Very few radical slices. My shots even got *better* by the third basket!

My concentration was good today. I took each shot as it came despite a series or two of poor shots. I was able to regain my poise due to focus. I let nothing distract me. Using a 5-iron, most of the balls that I hit well sailed about 120 yards.

I feel very positive today. I see my reading dovetailing with my practice. The reading is less academic as I learn to apply stuff to my actual swing.

Her swings were smooth and effortless. It was a perfect demonstration of the power of proper technique. Swing that club the right way and even a petite girl can wallop a golf ball.

Toward the end I felt a consistency develop. I set up in the same spot, in the same way in order to really set a groove. I felt that I'd achieved a trend and a control that hadn't been there before.

Too many times my swings have been unfocused. They've been Hail Mary-type things without a real focused effort that in turn yields a feeling that the swing is on track and the ball will be hit cleanly. This requires positive thinking on top of sound fundamental setup and backswing. I mean *really thinking* and *focusing* throughout the swing. Not simply pulling the trigger with a prayer *(Oh, well. Here it goes!),* but a flow of concentration that carries from setup to takeaway to backswing.

My stamina must be improving. I hit about 100 balls today and my last basket was the best by far.

So many positive signs:
1) Straighter shots
2) More consistency
3) More stamina
4) Better *focus* that yielded a

5) Better *feel* that yielded a
6) Positive frame of mind.

6-29: My Wife Tries

I took Kathleen with me, and she hit some balls, too. It was her first time. Although it was a sunny Sunday afternoon, only two others were using the grassy side of the range. One young lady was particularly talented. Stroke after stroke she hit her balls cleanly and precisely. Her swings were smooth and effortless. It was a perfect demonstration of the power of proper technique. Swing that club the right way and even a petite girl can wallop a golf ball.

Before we came to the range I showed Kathleen the grip, the stance and a point or two about the swing. I didn't want to put her off with alotta info up front so I kept it simple. I was thinking that it would be grand for her to just hit the ball. Actually she was reluctant to try so I was careful not to unload all the stuff that I'd been force-feeding myself over the last several weeks. There's nothing more annoying than a know-it-all. Especially a know-it-all spouse.

That's one thousand six hundred and seventy times I've stood over, stared at, pulled back from and whacked at a golf ball. I've entered a new realm and I think ... it's OK.

To her credit, she hit the ball nearly every time she swung. I don't think she whiffed or hit the turf more than twice out of 20 swings. Every ball went straight and a couple even met the sweetspot with her 8-iron. Sure, her swing was a little wobbly, but because her grip and setup were solid, she was able to meet the ball. She did a whole lot better than I did my first time!

After a while she decided to take a breather. "I think I better quit while I'm ahead," she said, and I knew exactly what she was talking about. Whether it's a last wave, a final run down the slopes or a final drive on the range, it's nice to end on a high note if possible.

With my 6-iron I hit about 40 balls and did about as well as yesterday. I felt confident and comfortable. When I did miss, I was able to settle down, make the right adjustments and hit the next shot. Some slicing, but not bad. I was happy to send several balls in the right direction.

I topped the last ball in my pile, so true to form, I went back to the ball

> *I discovered that in order to just begin learning I had to commit to the learning process and forget about rapid progress.*

dispenser to get just a few more in order to end the day with a solid shot. The machine spit out half a bucket, however, and I ended up with a lot more balls than I wanted. When Kathleen saw my new collection of golf balls, she came over to lend a hand. "If I want to leave before Monday, I better help you with those," she said.

Again, she hit well and even sent one on the fly to the 50-yard marker. I managed to hit the remaining balls in a respectable manner, and we called it a day.

INVENTORY OF RESULTS TO DATE

33 Sessions and 1,670 Swings

June was a full month of range work. Swinging only irons, mostly the 5 and 6. I bought my first set of clubs on May 5. I think I went to the range about three times before I got serious with this diary business, beginning June 13. From that day, I took note of each practice and wrote about the experience as you see here. That's a total of about 18 sessions for the month.

Before I bought my clubs, I hit twice in December and about 13 times, including the five professional lessons, in the fall. Before then I hit only once about 10 years previously.

May/June	18 sessions
December	2 sessions
October	5 pro lessons
	7 sessions
December	1 session

Total sessions:	*33 sessions*

If I averaged 50 balls a session, that makes 1,650 balls.

I probably swung nearly 1,670 times since I missed the ball at least 20 times.

> *I had to learn to be a student before I became a student.*

That's one thousand six hundred and seventy times I've stood over, stared at, pulled back from and whacked at a golf ball.

I've entered a new realm and I think ... it's OK.

Lessons and Learning How to Learn

I received the aforementioned five professional lessons plus three lessons from friends. The professional lessons were useful because I rubbed shoulders with a pro for the first time and learned a bit about technique and a whole lot about attitude (I CAINT HEAR YOOO!). The lessons from friends were not as crisply professional, but they weren't bad either. In fact, one of those "friendly" lessons was as good if not better than the ones I paid for.

I think the real value of the professional lessons was just meeting up with a pro I liked and who really seemed to care. Not to disparage what he actually tried to teach me, but I hardly remember what he did teach me as far as technique. I honestly think that in the beginning I was so anxious to hit the ball well that very little sunk in. And that was my fault. I wasn't ready to *absorb*. I wasn't ready to do that until recently. Back in October, I had no idea that the learning curve in this game was so long and steep. I thought that I'd be able to pick up the swing and hit the ball within a short period of time.

I discovered that in order to just *begin* learning I had to *commit* to the learning process and forget about rapid progress. I had to realize that nothing in my life had prepared me to take up golf. I had to learn to be a student before I became a student. Looking back at this point, I can see that the early lessons and sessions were so many poundings I endured. I had to have all the pride beaten out of me before I settled down to approach this game with a true willingness to *respect golf* and, therefore, a *willingness to learn* its fundamentals.

I'm learning stuff now because I'm open to it, and I realize that I have a long road to travel. Without the burden of pride, I'm able to pick up things easier through my reading and practice sessions. More importantly, I'm having *fun* with it.

Reading All About It

In the last two months I've read or partially read about 15 books on golf, seven magazines that had golfing tips and one tiny booklet. I watched one golfing video. Of this material, I found maybe five books useful, two or three particularly useful, and one magazine article very useful.

At first all this stuff was mind boggling, but now, with more than a few swings under my belt, I'm beginning to draw the connections. Make no mistake, it's still somewhat overwhelming because of the sheer volume and variety of the instructional material, yet now I know what I'm looking for. I'm beginning to know my own game and I know what I need.

Make no mistake, it's still somewhat overwhelming because of the sheer volume and variety of the instructional material, yet now I know what I'm looking for. I'm beginning to know my own game and I know what I need.

> *You realize somewhere down the line that not only must you hit the ball consistently, but you must also hit it at or near a target!*

Second, it's less confusing now because I've come to realize that most of the literature is about the same things. Most of the differences are a matter of approach, style and detail. Actually it's kinda interesting to read through the various viewpoints. You know, there's nothing wrong with alotta info if you know how to plug into it!

I'm doing most of my technical learning through the literature. I'm sure the lessons were valuable on a subconscious level, but like I said, I don't remember them being technically useful. I recall some things, but I was too fat-headed for the lessons to really sink in. I also think that instructors sometimes forget that they're dealing with beginners, and they try to impart too much too soon. They forget what tiny little golfing minds we have. Again, students must be ready to be students before anything can be learned.

Results of 1,670 Swings

Besides learning to be a student, this is what I have learned and *feel comfortable executing* to date:

These parts of the *Basic Swing*:
1) Grip
2) Establishing the proper distance from the ball
3) Stance and posture
4) Takeaway
5) Parts of the backswing
6) Parts of the downswing and follow-through

I have also achieved:
7) A knowledge of the equipment
8) A knowledge of the game and its history
9) A feel for what might be the proper attitude and mental state to assume around this game

The Bottom Line

At this point, I'm fairly confident that I can hit the ball straight and up in the air with a 5-iron. It's safe to assume that I can also do the same with the loftier irons numbered from 6 through 10 (because they're even easier to hit).

What's Next?

My weaknesses are vast, of course, but of immediate concern are:

1) *Gaining proficiency and confidence with my backswing and downswing.*

I'm just starting to examine things beyond the takeaway. At the moment I'm thinking about my hips leading the downswing. The thing is: you gotta have all the older stuff down to muscle memory in order to commit your mind to newer things. The older stuff has to keep up with the new in order for the whole swing to work. It can't be forgotten or left behind.

2) *Targeting my shots*

You realize somewhere down the line that not only must you hit the ball *consistently*, but you must also *hit it at or near a target!* After all, golf is a *target* game. Being a good hitter is only the means to this end.

3) *Gaining proficiency with the 3- and 4-irons as well as all the woods*

I have to say that this advice was very helpful. So often a friend's advice can be wearisome or even trouble. That's why it's almost universally recommended that a beginner seek professional help. But each session with this guy was great fun with good results.

The longer irons are difficult for everybody because they have flatter clubfaces and a nastier impact with the ball. The woods shouldn't be as great a problem, but we'll see.

> *Wow! It's so true: all you need is one, just one good shot to make your day. Because if you can hit the one, you can certainly hit another.*

4) I *think* that I can stumble through a game (have I said that before?) and I *think* I'm ready to try. Although I'm hardly an accomplished swinger and hitter, after 1,700 swings it might be time to tee off.

Why not?

7-9: Like Taking a Whiz?

I went surfing this morning and met up with a good friend who had once given me an insightful lesson last fall. We met at a range later on and again his pointers were right on the money.

He watched me hit a few with the 6-iron and suggested I address the ball with it smack in the middle of my stance. I had been lining the ball more toward my left heel. He also had me step closer and relax my arms. "It's just like taking a whiz," he said as he gripped his club and demonstrated how he marked his distance from the ball. Finally, he asked me to turn my right hand a bit more counterclockwise in my grip. The result: Boom! Up and away with only a fade for 150 yards. I did even better with clubs from his new set of Pings.

I also tried my 3-wood and did OK. Man, it really *drives* when you connect! Many slices, however, due to a backswing that travels too far and bounces.

Overall, a very good time. I will play a game with him and his wife this Friday afternoon. Nine holes.

Here, again, I have to say that this advice was very helpful. So often a friend's advice can be wearisome or even trouble. That's why it's almost universally recommended that a beginner seek professional help. But each session with this guy was great fun with good results. Maybe I'm just lucky to have a friend who happens to be an excellent coach who shows up exactly when I need precisely the kind of advice he's so capable of giving. He figures I'm simply more relaxed because I'm not shelling out for a pro's time.

At any rate, it's wonderful to gain tips that really work from an in-the-flesh coaching experience. For the most part, my instruction has come from golfing literature and trial and error. Not that that's bad. It's just a little lonely sometimes.

A perfect day for golf. Overcast and sprinkles.

7-11: One Good Shot

Hit about 40 balls. Used the Whizzer's Stance from yesterday and socked a few OK until Mr. Slice arrived. Fidgeted, made an adjustment or two and belted one beauty for 160 yards. It was so perfectly straight (I'm used to at least a 25-yard fade) that I stopped and stared bug-eyed with open jaw.

Wow! It's so true: all you need is *one*, just one good shot to make your day. Because if you can hit the one, you can certainly hit another. Then one day, maybe one day soon, you'll hit a few in a row. And isn't *that* a tasty vision!

I haven't been wearing my glove and have suffered no ill effects. The glove feels good but it's nice to feel the grip with bare hand, too. Goes to show that if you hold the club with only a firm (not tight) grip you won't get blisters.

The Japanese Video Golfers set up shop next to me and put on their usual clinic. All they need is a sound track and matching sequin outfits.

They're that good (in my eyes).

> *I swung and missed twice before I connected on the first tee. I was so pumped to be playing a real game of golf at last!*

It was like being kids again, trying to play out all nine holes before darkness fell.

7-12: Game #1: Pumped!

Today was the day. My debut on the links.

I met my instructor/buddy for a late afternoon nine holes. I had hit some balls earlier at a nearby range to warm up. My slice was so wicked that I got a little nervous about the actual game. The nervousness pretty much stuck with me, too, as I swung and missed *twice* before I connected on the first tee. I was so pumped to be playing a real game of golf at last!

I settled down fast, though, and had an absolutely terrific time. We had to play fast anyway since the sun was setting and I simply didn't have the time to choke.

Overall, I hit the ball pretty good, but with a slice on the long balls. I did OK with the shorter irons around the green and my putting was just fine. We didn't keep score, but I'd say that I played around two over par for maybe five of the holes. Some of the holes were out of control because I hit trees or landed in traps. I did take some extra hits under my friend's tutelage in order to learn and sharpen technique. On my last hole, and in the dark, I hit a 5-iron (my friend's) to the green! I should have been able to par the hole after that, but I just missed my putt for the par 3 and had to settle for a bogie (one stroke over par).

I had been looking forward to this game for quite some time (like over six months!) but I'm still somewhat amazed at how excited I was and still am. The last time I felt this stoked was when I rediscovered longboard surfing over two years ago. Man, I can't wait to get out there again!

Lessons Learned

What sticks in my mind is swinging and missing the ball with my first two strokes! I need to calm down, relax and focus. Just let that swing happen. The slice also needs to be addressed (again!) somehow.

Fun We Had
Way too much of this! Combination of crew and conditions. Nobody pushing us from behind. It was like being kids again, trying to play out all nine holes before darkness fell. Running from ball to ball without worrying about hitting a perfect shot (although so many were not bad!).

7-15: Game #2: Executive Jogging

Played nine holes with another friend at a local executive course. Most of the course is made up of par 3 holes. This game moved much quicker than my first due to the shorter distances.

I hit the ball up, but Mr. Slice is back. We didn't keep score and when we weren't pushed from behind we hit second and even third balls for practice. In order to keep up the pace with all these balls, we jogged from lie to lie, which I like. Who said golf had to be a walk in the park?

I got my first par *ever(!)* and played one over on a couple other holes. I lost one ball.

Afterward we split a bucket of balls and hit some on the range. I practiced with all the clubs and still hit with a slice or a fade. The only high point was my 3-iron. I hit that OK off a tee and was encouraged because I'll need to use it on those shorter holes. We were pretty tired by the end of that and, of course, hitting miserably.

We watched one guy warming up who just creamed the ball *on target* with every club. He had this Quasimodo stance and crouch that would make an instructor wince, but still he was long and accurate.

He also wore a Hawaiian shirt, cute little white shorts, a Panama hat and had (get this) skunk skin covers on his woods. Looking like that, the guy had better be good!

> *Poor Reggie was out there with a swing that wouldn't connect with a basketball and not once felt the joy of a solid hit. The importance of developing the Basic Swing before you play a game couldn't have hit home with me any more dramatically.*

He stood about 5 feet 6 inches and was built like a fire plug. He also wore a Hawaiian shirt, cute little white shorts, a Panama hat and had (get *this*) *skunk skin* covers on his woods. Looking like that, the guy had better be good!

7-16: Game #3: Crashing in on My Own

Took off on my own late this afternoon in hopes of finding the course empty. I hit a bucket first just to get warmed up and hit the ball very well, but it looks like Mr. Slice is here to stay for a while. Every ball curved and landed in the same spot. At least I'm consistent! Went to the pro shop, slapped down nine bucks and headed out.

Still jittery for the first hole or two, yet I connected and moved it along. A fellow and his wife were ahead of me and for the first time I had to slow my game. Round about the third hole they disappeared and I ran into two guys moving even slower. On holes running next to each other I hit one into their fairway and they hit balls into mine. We cracked our balls through the trees to get back on track and laughed at each other as we crossed paths.

As I teed up on the fourth hole, they were still poking around the fairway ahead and kindly waved me to hit. Compensating for my slice, I aimed toward the left but it went fairly straight this time and screamed directly at the fellows standing there. They saw it and laughed as it settled in a good lie about 100 yards from the green. Then I hit a 6-iron smack into a greenside bunker. I ran up and offered to join them as I was right on top of them anyway and they cheerfully assented. My sand shot was almost perfect, and I think I holed out in four strokes giving me a par (I wasn't really keeping score).

My new partners were very impressed and couldn't believe that this was only my third game. I told them that I'd spent a *long* time on the range. I discovered why the fellows were moving so slow when I saw one of them, Reggie, take a few strokes and muff each one. He hadn't played in three years and had *never practiced on the range(!)*. He had no game at all.

The other guy, Mattie, was pretty good, though, and I was happy to play along. Actually, my game is better with company and Mattie commented that his concentration improves when he plays with others as well.

So we moved along, commenting on club selection and sharing tips (from him to me) about how to hit certain shots. I was all ears, of course, and grateful for the information.

On the next hole I cursed a lousy shot and Mattie said, "Golf is the only game where you can have fun on a bad day. An older guy told me that the other day and I think about that a lot." This, of course, was a great piece of advice so I settled down, relaxed, and decided to enjoy the company of new golfing friends, the game, the empty course and the evening.

We reached the last hole as the sun disappeared and Mattie landed a terrific tee shot next to the flag. I hit two balls as my first was poor, but the second was not much better. One of my pitches was pretty, though, and although my putts were mediocre, that one stroke made me feel good.

"I'm sorry, but you've become a golfing widow," I said. She just looked at me like a wife does sometimes.

All in all not a bad session. Taking Mattie's advice to the limit, perhaps no golfing experience is really bad if it's fun you're after. I hit a couple woods I liked and a couple pitches,

> *Man, I'm a Beginner.*
> *A rank Kook at this*
> *game. I'm a certified*
> *Hacker and entitled*
> *to careening about*
> *the course on a walk*
> *or a run, hitting as*
> *many balls as I want,*
> *with whatever club*
> *I want, whenever I*
> *want, as long as*
> *I don't interfere with*
> *another golfer, bean*
> *anybody or club*
> *someone to death.*

too. I parred maybe two holes and hit my best sand shot ever. Most important, I moved the ball along. Although each shot wasn't good or even hit up, I still covered ground, more than kept up and didn't lose any balls.

In short, I'm confident that I can play. Certainly not par golf or bogie golf but *in-the-game* golf (I still don't even wanna keep score). I now hit the ball all the time (I don't miss much anymore), I can usually hit in the general direction of the flag, and I can count on a good stroke or two to keep me from totally losing it on almost every hole. All those hours on the range are paying off. Poor Reggie was out there with a swing that wouldn't connect with a basketball and not once felt the joy of a solid hit. The importance of developing the *Basic Swing* before you play a game couldn't have hit home with me any more dramatically.

I got home after eight and Kathleen was mildly disappointed because she had rustled up dinner two hours earlier. "I'm sorry, but you've become a golfing widow," I said. She just looked at me like a wife does sometimes.

Picking Stuff Up

The game doesn't have to be rigid (thank goodness!). If you have the time and the course to yourself, why not hit extra balls? Heck, bend the rules and *play*. Don't keep score or worry about penalties. Keep hitting balls and experimenting with all the clubs. Find out what works. If someone is slow in front of you, skip a hole and play on through if it isn't bothering anybody. Or team up with them. *Keep moving.* At this point it's the *playing* that's important. Hitting balls in different lies with different clubs. The only scoring I do is per hole and that's in my head. I don't use a card. I aim for par but if that doesn't happen because I'm hitting trees, muffing the longer shots, digging in the sand or losing balls, *who cares?*

Man, I'm a *Beginner*. A rank *Kook* at this game. I'm a certified *Hacker* and entitled to careening about the course on a walk or a run, hitting as many balls as I want, with whatever club I want, whenever I want, as long as I don't interfere with another golfer, bean anybody or club someone to death. Hey, enjoy it while you can! Because if you keep at it, you'll get good one day, and when you get good you'll create expectations for yourself. And then it's all over. The Kook will eventually become an Average Golfer and start worrying about breaking 100 for 18 holes, then 90, then 80, then ... but I'm getting waaaaay ahead of myself here.

7-18: Losing It, "That's Golf!" and Frank Sinatra

Wanted to play a game but as it was getting late I opted for the range. Drew 50 balls from the ball dispenser and proceeded to miss hit about 49 of them. Awful! I was just plain awful! I hit one 6-iron that came close to being a good shot. The rest were slices and toppers. My God! I thought the topper days were long gone!

I've come to learn that the tiny phrase "That's Golf!" is the official slogan, mantra and healing balm for our game.

I finished and on the way out I saw Tom, my instructor, who wanted my business card in order to talk about a book idea. I finally told him about this book (I had kept it a secret in order to go through the beginner's learning curve as authentically as possible) and I said that I'd probably need some help. He said that he'd just confuse things.

> *"Not so fast! You've got time to hit a golf ball the right way," he commanded and like a good little boy (it was like I was 12 years old) I came back and fired away at one more.*

I told him about my first games and the lousy day I just had on the driving range. He was enthusiastic and encouraging, as always, and said *"That's Golf!"* I've come to learn that the tiny phrase *That's Golf!* is the official slogan, mantra and healing balm for our game. Much like *That's Life!* are the two mighty little words that have seen Frank Sinatra through his various trials and tribulations.

I had a miserable day of surfing, too, so it was a poor day for athletics in general. To my credit, I wasn't mad about the day or even that concerned. Heck, it was just another day and I knew I could perform well enough (surfing, golfing, whatever) when the stars were lined correctly, so I concentrated on the next and last performance of the day, which was about the only thing left that I was very confident about: eating dinner.

7-20: Game #4: Same Old Slice

With Kathleen along on this balmy, late afternoon trek, I play about as good as I had been playing. Slow to start, I began to hit the ball better by the third hole, but still with the big, looping slice. I was so bad that I aimed off to the left just to keep the ball in play. Of course, that only worked when the slice was *on*. When I hit the ball *straight* I was either in the trees, the next fairway or completely out of the park. One ball screamed over the heads of two little old ladies strolling on a nearby nature trail. *I've got to do something about this!*

I managed a couple of pars and some of my shots were OK. It was still a good time and quite pleasant with the late setting sun. Kathleen was impressed with the beauty and serenity of the setting (nobody was about) and said she now understood some of the game's appeal. She brought along a book and read calmly while I set up for shots, stroked and cursed.

We started so late that by the seventh hole it was getting dark. I teamed up with a guy who jumped the fence and he gave me a pointer or two on our last hole. He was pretty good and could really hit a straight shot (man, I'm into straight shots!). Off the tee, he hit a beautiful 5-wood while I belted one into the trees. I took mine out of the woods and hit a nice 7-iron onto the green! My best shot of the day. Better, even, than his, which landed a bit short. We holed out with nothing but the clubhouse lights to see by.

He told me that I was slicing because I was turning too much of my body into the backswing. That I should be rotating my shoulders around a stable spine (as if I didn't know that!). I felt that he was on to something because it did feel like I was swaying during the swing. (Again, an example of the friendly advice from strangers that is given and taken so freely.)

7-21: My Guardian Angel

Keen to cure my slicing habit, I headed out to the driving range. I fiddled with my stance and my grip but nothing really worked. After about 10 lousy shots I looked up and met the eyes of an older fellow sitting on a bench nearby.

"How goes it?" he asked with some sort of East Coast drawl.

"Oh, well. My slice is killing me. I'm just trying to hit a straight ball."

"You're arm isn't straight," he replied immediately with some authority. "Get that arm straight." He pronounced *arm* like *aaam* so it had to be New England.

> *I wasn't ready to dive into the drink, but I was certainly entertaining the thought of throwing my clubs into the nearest water hazard.*

> *Thank you, Earl, wherever you are. I'll think of you every time I hear a bell ring. Or better yet, whenever I hit the dang ball straight!*

Although somewhat annoyed at the old man's strident tone, I realized he was right, and I straightened out the left arm. To my surprise and irritation, it felt very awkward. It dawned on me that it was awkward because I'd completely forgotten about this very basic fundamental. I was swinging the club, and apparently had been swinging the club for some time, like a baseball bat.

"You're swinging it like a baseball bat. You don't swing it like a baseball bat," he said like an echo to my thoughts. He got up and demonstrated with his club. "Your left arm and your club should form a straight line." Again, basic stuff that I knew but had simply stopped doing. I tried it and it felt so strange that I knew I had been floundering with some bad habits for a while.

On cue he says, "You see, you've been nurturing a bad habit here. Go ahead and hit one." I do and I hit a grounder. "You topped it," he said. Well, no kidding.

I hit another and it went fairly straight. It was still awkward because, by golly, I had been holding and extending the club all wrong for weeks, but I knew the old guy was on to something. I settled in for a couple more shots and it began to feel better and better.

"Now turn your left hand over some," he commanded. I rotated my left hand a good half inch clockwise. "Get those creases pointed toward your right shoulder. Good. Try again." I hit another with just a slight fade. Then I looked at my watch and realized that I was late for a movie date with Kathleen.

"Thanks!" I said. "I gotta go but it was great meeting you ..."

"*Not so fast!* You've got time to hit a golf ball the right way," he commanded and like a good little boy (it was like I was 12 years old) I came back and fired away at one more.

And lo! The ball flew-eth high, straight and true. The best shot I've had in ... my life?(!)

"I bet that was the best ball you've hit in quite some time," he said in absolute confidence because he was obviously able to read my every thought.

I thanked him profusely, found out his name was Earl, that he was 73 years old with heart problems, that he was just visiting and would be gone tomorrow. Then I lit out.

It was sorta like the movies, you know? In the Christmas classic, *It's a Great Life,* Jimmy Stewart jumps off a bridge and his guardian angel descends in the nick of time to save his life and eventually convinces him to carry on. Well, Old Earl was my guardian angel today. Although my situation was a lot less critical than Jimmy Stewart's, his timely appearance and convincing approach to my troubles was no less a godsend. I wasn't ready to dive into the drink, but I was certainly entertaining the thought of throwing my clubs into the nearest water hazard.

Thank you, Earl, wherever you are. I'll think of you every time I hear a bell ring. Or better yet, whenever I hit the dang ball straight!

7-25: Game #5: Oh Well

I hit some balls very well while warming up on the range. But I think I hit a few too many because once I got out on the course, my game fell apart pretty fast.
Got out there late and played for free. Started out well enough, but as I continued to play, the slice kicked in and pretty soon I couldn't even

Dealing with golf's afflictions can be very similar to dealing with life's addictions. There are no "cures" and one must be prepared to take the game one day at a time.

Now, I'm much too wary to think for an instant that I've found a cure, but the above procedure helped me today.

get the ball off the ground. Some good short shots, though, and I sunk a 15-foot putt. I parred one hole.

I must be slow. Two fellows were hot on my tail the whole time. As it was getting dark, I skipped over to the 18th hole to finish up. I lost a shot in the water and barely escaped a shot from a party playing behind me. They were in carts and moved up fast. I just quit and moved on since they were there legitimately, and I wasn't playing worth a nickel anyway.

7-27: Slicing (But My Wife Thinks I'm Great)
Hit 40 balls at the range just to get some hitting time in. Hit some straight. Mostly sliced. Brought KW. She thinks I do great (right!).

7-28: Slicing (But I Hit Four Drives Straight)
On the range again. Hit 100 balls. Mostly irons. Mostly slices. Hit six balls with the driver and hit four of them very well. Go figure.

7-29: Slicing (With Some Fades)
Back on the range. Another 100 balls. Hit two straight. Not that they're all slices, but they all fade (veer right). What a bloody fix. I do not want to play another game with this problem.

7-30: Slicing (But at Least Connecting)
Although I'm still troubled by a slice, I am hitting the ball solidly and consistently. I missed a ball and realized that I hadn't done that in quite some time.

7-31: Breakthrough!
Much improvement today. Hit all my clubs well. The straightest shots I've had in quite some time. Maybe I'm settling into a new level. I can only hope after hitting the ball so poorly for so long. What's different?

The Procedure

I've fiddled with my grip in different ways for about two weeks. What worked today was a left hand turned in clockwise a bit more than what had come to feel normal. In the setup, I laid the clubface flat on the ground and gripped the club with my left thumb on top of the handle. When I turned the club clockwise in order to square the blade, my left hand was well over and "strong" in the grip. I scooched the hand counterclockwise just a bit to feel comfortable and simply folded the right hand over it.

This grip somehow forced me to set up with a straight left arm. With the straight, extended left arm and club, I settled into the proper distance from the ball. I also aligned myself to the target line with the ball a certain distance off my left foot depending on the club, of course.

I did a final settling in and checked for lower right shoulder, straight arm and proper positioning to the ball.

My stance was flexed, not crouched. Comfortably spaced and not too wide.

There was a point where it felt about right.

I eyed the ball and thought: Square Blade On The Ball (S-BOB). I took a practice takeaway, came back in and checked for S-BOB.

Still eyeing the ball, I pulled the trigger thinking S-BOB. The takeaway was drawn back low, straight, smooth and steady (LS-3). I was thinking S-BOB all the way. I pulled through the ball thinking S-BOB, S-BOB, S-BOB!

> *Because even though you might lick one problem this day, you're bound to spring a leak somewhere else the next.*

Now, I'm much too wary to think for an instant that I've found a cure, but the above procedure helped me *today*. I can *only hope* that it will work tomorrow. Dealing with golf's afflictions can be very similar to dealing with life's addictions. There are no "cures" and one must be prepared to take the game one day at a time. Because even though you might lick one problem this day, you're bound to spring a leak somewhere else the next. It's really something of a mystery and therein lies the challenge, the romance and the occasional heartbreak of the sport.

(It's Never) The End!

(Mostly)

Early Days

A Golfing Timeline

1457-1966: From James II to Jack

Golf had its ancient beginnings in more than one place, however, Scotland is where it truly took root and developed.

1457: Golf has become so popular in Scotland that it begins to interfere with compulsory archery training. The game is prohibited by the Scot's Parliament of King James II.

1471: Parliament under James III also forbids the play of golf.

1491: Parliament under James IV again forbids golf.

1503-1506: But the King sneaks in a round! Records indicate that James IV plays golf with the Earl of Bothwell.

1592: The Town Council of Edinburgh prohibits the play of golf on Sundays.

1603: The invention of gunpowder makes archery obsolete as a weapon of war. It makes laws prohibiting golf due to its interference with archery training obsolete as well. King James VI appoints William Mayne as Royal Club-Maker.

1618: It's official: James VI allows the playing of golf on Sundays after attending church.

1633: King Charles I commands that his subjects not be molested for playing golf as long as they attend church first on Sundays.

1744: The Honorable Company of Edinburgh Golfers is established in Edinburgh, Scotland: the first ever golfing society.

1754: The St. Andrews Society of Golfers, now known as the Royal and Ancient Club of St. Andrews, is formed. It has been in continuous operation ever since and is considered the spiritual home of golf.

Over the next 100 years, a number of clubs are established, mostly in Scotland.

1778: The Blackheath Golf Club near London becomes the first golf club in England.

1810: The first account of ladies golf is made at the Musselburgh Golf Club in Scotland.

1814: The first golf course on the European continent is laid out by two Scot officers in Pau, France, after the Battle of Orthez.

1829: A golf club is formed in Calcutta, India.

1842: A golf club is formed in Bombay, India.

1845: The first gutta-percha ball is made by the Rev. Dr. Robert Adams Patterson. Gutta-percha is the gum produced from certain Malayan trees. These balls replace balls made from feathers and leather. Gutta-percha balls are easier and faster to make and perform better than the old, stuffed feather balls.

1854: The clubhouse at St. Andrews is completed and King William IV confers to the club a new title: The Ancient and Royal Club of St. Andrews. The club becomes the epicenter and showcase for golf. It is here that the first rules of golf are written. St. Andrews has served as the headquarters for the governing body of golf in Great Briton to this day. Hugh Lyon Playfair, the town provost, and Allan Robertson, the first celebrity golfer, create a groundswell of interest in the game through contests and promotions.

1857: The first National Golf Club Championship is held at St. Andrews.

1860: The First British Open Championship is held at Prestwick.

1864: The first seaside course in England is laid out at Westward Ho.

1865: A second course is created in London on the Wimbledon Commons.

1868: The first ladies golf clubs are established at St. Andrews (Scotland), Westward Ho (England) and North Devon (England).

1869: The Royal Liverpool Golf Club lays out the now-famous course at Hoylake.

1873: The Royal Montreal Club establishes the first club and course in North America.

1881: The Royal Belfast Club, one of the first clubs in Ireland, is established at the Kinnegar.

1887: Ardent golfer Lord Balfour is appointed Chief Secretary of Ireland. His fondness for the game is much publicized and helps to popularize the game in England.

1887: The first permanent golf club in the United States is established in Foxsburg, Pennsylvania. There is evidence, however, that golf was played in America as early as 1779 in a number of states.

1888: The St. Andrews Club is formed in the home of John Reid in Yonkers, New York.

By 1894 close to 50 clubs spring up across the United States.

1893: The first British Ladies Championships is held at Lytham and St. Annes.

Between 1890 and 1895 the number of golf courses worldwide grew from 387 to 1,280.

1894: The Amateur Golf Association of the United States is formed in New York at the Calumet Club. Henry O. Tallmadge invites five leading clubs to send representatives to the club to form the governing body of golf that will eventually become the United States Golf Association (USGA).

1895: The above association sponsors its first three annual championships: the Men's Amateur and the Men's Open at the Newport Golf Club in Newport, Rhode Island and the Women's Amateur at Meadow Brook Golf Club in Hempstead, New York.

1900: A.G. Spalding Company sponsors the exhibition tour of Briton's Harry Vardon in the United States. Vardon was then considered the greatest golfer in the world and his tour sparks great interest in the game of golf.

1902: Dr. Coburn Haskell develops the rubber golf ball, the first major golf innovation for 50 years.

1911: John J. McDermott is the first American to win the U.S. Open at the Chicago Golf Club in Wheaton, Illinois. Up to this point the championship has been dominated by British golfers.

1914: Harry Vardon wins his sixth British Open.

From 1894 to 1914 three golfers known as "The Triumvirate" win 16 British Open titles. They are Harry

Vardon, James Braid and John H. Taylor.

1916: The Professional Golfers' Association (PGA) is formed.

By 1920, membership in the USGA had grown to 477 clubs.

1923: Bobby Jones wins the U.S. Open and the first of his 13 major championships.

1927: Walter Hagen wins his fifth PGA Championship.

Between 1920 and 1930 Bobby Jones wins 13 major championships and Walter Hagen wins 11.

1929: The supremacy of American golfers is demonstrated during the British Open. Of the top 10 golfers in the match, eight, including the winner, Walter Hagen, are American.

1930: Bobby Jones wins the British Amateur, the British Open, the U.S. Amateur and the U.S. Open. This feat is dubbed the "Grand Slam" and is still considered one of the greatest feats in golf history.

1930: There are 5,700 golf courses in the United States including 4,450 private clubs, 500 municipal courses and 700 privately owned public fee courses. There are 2,000 courses in the British Empire and a total of 9,000 worldwide.

1931: The Royal and Ancient Club of St. Andrews approves the use of steel shafted clubs.

1931-1935: The Depression takes its toll. Club membership in the USGA drops from 1,154 to 767. Of the tournaments that survive, many must cut the prize purse.

1932: Gene Sarazen wins both the U.S. Open and the British Open. Sarazen will go on to win seven major titles.

1934: The first Masters Tournament is held at the Augusta National Golf Club in Augusta, Georgia.

1936: The USGA reports an increase in membership. The PGA announces that professionals will compete for more than $100,000 during the year.

By the end of the 1930s some of golf's greatest names have begun to make their mark, including Byron Nelson, Sam Snead and Ben Hogan.

1936-1946: Byron Nelson wins 50 championships. In 1945 he wins 11 consecutive championships.

1946: The PGA holds 45 tournaments with more than $600,000 in total cash awards.

1946: The first women's professional tournament, the United States Women's Open Championship, is held in Spokane, Washington.

1949: Sam Snead wins the Masters, the National PGA Championship, the Western Open, the North and South Open, the Vardon Trophy (for achieving the lowest scoring average) and is the year's top money winner.

1953: Ben Hogan wins the Masters Tournament, the U.S. Open and the British Open.

1954: The U.S. Open is televised for the first time.

1958: There are 5,700 golf courses in the United States. This is the same number of courses as there were in 1931 before the Depression took its toll.

1959: Professional golfers play for more than $1 million in total cash prizes in PGA sponsored tournaments. More than four million Americans play 10 rounds or more for a grand total of 81 million rounds.

1960: Television and President Eisenhower's enthusiasm for the game take golf to even greater levels of popularity. There are now 6,011 courses in the United States including 3,162 private, 1,997 semiprivate and 852 municipal courses.

1962: Baseball is the only sport televised more than golf.

1963: There are six million golfers in the United States, including 700,000 women.

1964: There are now nine million golfers playing on 8,500 courses in the United States. Almost $130 million is spent on equipment.

1964: Arnold Palmer wins his fourth Masters Tournament. He now has won seven major championships.

1964: Mickey Wright wins her fourth U.S. Women's Open, is the leading money winner for the fourth consecutive time and wins a total of 11 tournaments.

1965: There are 8,332 golf courses in the United States and more than 10 million golfers.

1965: Jack Nicklaus wins his second Masters with a record score of 271. South Africa's Gary Player wins the U.S. Open and becomes only the third golfer to win the three leading championships of the United States.

1966: Jack Nicklaus becomes the first golfer to win back-to-back Masters Tournaments. He has won six major victories and all four of the major professional titles.

There are now 8,672 golf courses in the United States upon which about 176 million rounds of golf are played.

Flash forward to the new century: There are now 26.2 million golfers in the United States at more than 16,057 golf facilities who spend $24.3 billion in green fees and golf equipment each year. *

*www.golfchannelsolutions.com/markets/usa

Glossary

Ace- Hole in one. Making a hole in one stroke.

Address- The position a golfer takes at the ball in order to set up or prepare to swing.

Approach- A stroke played to the green or pin.

Apron- The grass border surrounding the green.

Away- Refers to the farthest ball from the hole. The golfer whose ball is "away" shoots first.

Back Side- The last nine holes of an 18-hole course.

Backspin- The reverse spin imparted to a ball that causes it to stop on the green.

Backswing- That part of the swing that draws back from the ball, up and over the head.

Basic Swing- The precise and coordinated method of stroking a golf ball that includes proper grip, posture and swing.

Birdie- One stroke under par.

Bogey- One stroke over par.

Bunker- A sand trap.

Carry- The distance a ball travels from where its struck to where it first hits the turf.

Casual Water- A temporary pool of water. Not a water hazard.

Chip Shot- A low trajectory shot taken near the green.

Choke- A grip made farther down the handle than normal.

Closed Clubface- The clubface is turned in or toward the target.

Closed Stance- The right foot is pulled back from the target line and/or the left foot is placed over the target line.

Clubface- The front of the clubhead.

Clubhead- The business end of the club opposite the handle.

Course- The entire field of play. A course comprises nine or 18 holes. Each hole has a tee, a fairway and a putting green.

Cup- The hole in the putting green.

Divot- A chunk of turf dug out by a club.

Drive- The shot made from a tee.

Driver- The No. 1 wood. Used for maximum distance.

Eagle- Two strokes under par.

Fade- A shot that turns slightly from left to right at the end of its flight.

Fairway- The area between tee and putting green on each hole.

Fat Shot- Hitting the ground before hitting the ball.

Follow-Through- That part of the swing that continues after the ball has been struck.

Fore- Look Out!

Fringe- The grass border surrounding the green. Also the apron.

Front Side- The first nine holes of an 18-hole course.

Grain- Refers to the direction the grass lies or grows on a putting green.

Green Fee- The cost of playing a particular course.

Grip- Refers to the handle on a club or the manner in which it's held.

Hacker- An unskilled golfer. Most of us.

Handicap- The number of strokes a player receives to

adjust his scoring ability to the ability of a scratch or zero-handicap golfer.

Hazard- A bunker (sand trap) or a standing area of water on the course.

Hole- The hole in a putting green or the area of play consisting of a tee, fairway and putting green.

Hook- A shot that curves to the left of target.

Interlock Grip- A variation of the overlap grip in which the little finger of the right hand is intertwined with the first finger of the left.

Iron- Club with a slim (compared to woods) metal head. These clubs are numbered 1-9 and also include wedges. They are classified as long (1-3), middle (4-6) or short (7-9) irons.

Lie- The position of the ball on the ground.

Links- A name for a golf course.

Lip- The top edge of a hole or cup.

Long Game- Those shots that require distance.

Loft- The elevation a ball takes in the air. Also refers to the angle of the clubface.

Match Play- Competition based on hole total versus stroke total.

Mulligan- A second shot permitted in casual play.

Open Stance- The left foot is drawn back from the target line.

Open Clubface: The clubface is turned out or away from the target.

Overclubbing- Using a club that provides more distance than required.

Overlap Grip- The recommended knitted grip for holding a club.

Par- The standard for good performance. The designated number of strokes that a player should take for each hole or the entire course.

Penalty Stroke- A stroke added to a player's score for a rule violation.

Pin- The flag in the hole.

Pitch- A lofted shot taken close to the green.

Pitching Wedge- A club designed to make short lofted shots.

Playing Through- When a party is allowed to pass another party playing ahead.

Plugged Lie- A ball buried in a sand trap.

Pull- A ball that goes left of the target with little curving.

Push- A ball that goes right of the target with little curving.

Putt- A stroke of the ball on the putting green.

Putter- Club used to stroke the ball on the putting green.

Putting Green- That area at the end of each hole where a golfer sinks his putts.

Range- A practice area for hitting balls.

Rough- Areas of high grass surrounding the tee, fairway and putting green.

Round- Refers to 18 holes of play.

Run- The distance a ball rolls after it strikes the ground.

Sand Trap- A bunker.

Sand Wedge- A club designed to loft the ball out of bunkers.

Scratch- To play par golf.

Shank- To hit the ball on the lower shaft or hosel of the club.

Short Game- Chipping, pitching and putting.

Skulling- Hitting the ball at or above its center during a chip or pitch shot causing it to travel farther than desired.

Slice- A shot that curves to the right of the target.

Stroke- The act of swinging at the ball.

Stroke Play- Competition based on stroke totals. Medal play.

Sweetspot- The center of the clubface. The desired point of impact.

Swing- The stroke a golfer uses to hit the ball.

Takeaway- The first 18 inches or so of the backswing.

Target Line- The desired path from lie to target.

Tee- The wooden peg used to prop up the ball. Also that area of each hole where play begins.

Toe- The end of the clubface.

Top- To hit the ball above its center causing it to stay low or on the ground.

Underclubbing- Using a club that provides less distance than required.

Unplayable Lie- A ball positioned such that it can't be hit.

Wedge- A high-lofted iron used for short shots.

Whizzer's Stance- A colorful label for an effective way of determining distance from the ball at address.

Wood- A club with a large wooden or metal head used for longer distances.

Bibliography

Books

Casper, Billy. *The Good Sense of Golf*. Englewood Cliffs, New Jersey: Prentice-Hall, Inc., 1980.

Faulkner, Max. *Play Championship Golf All Your Life*. London, England: Pelham Books, 1972.

Gallwey, W. Timothy. *The Inner Game of Golf*. New York, New York: Random House, 1979.

Garber, Angus. *Golf Legends*. Stamford, Connecticut: Longmeadow Press, 1988.

Gibson, Nevin. *A Pictorial History of Golf*. New York, New York: A.S. Barnes and Company, 1968.

Golf Magazine. *Golf Magazine's Encyclopedia of Golf: The Complete Reference*. New York, New York: HarperCollins Publishers, 1993.

Hogan, Ben. *Five Lessons: The Modern Fundamentals of Golf*. New York, New York: Simon & Schuster, 1957.

Plumridge, Chris. *How to Play Golf*. Secaucus, New Jersey: Chartwell Books, Inc., 1979.

Snead, Sam. *Golf Begins at Forty*. New York, New York: The Dial Press, 1978.

Taylor, Dawson. *Inside Golf*. Chicago, Illinois: Contemporary Books, Inc., 1978.

Yogi, Count. *Five Simple Steps to Perfect Golf*. Los Angeles, California: North Publishing, 1973.

Magazines

Golf Digest. Trumbull, Connecticut: NYT Sports/Leisure Magazines.

Golf Lessons. New York, New York: Harris Publications, Inc.

Golf Magazine. New York, New York: Times Mirror Magazines.

Golf Tips. Los Angeles, California: Werner Publishing Corporation.

Petersen's Golfing. Los Angeles, California: Petersen Publishing Company.

Play Better Golf. New York, New York: Harris Publications, Inc.

Index

ZZZZZAP! This is just an interesting photo that had to find its way into the book.

Impact! At this point the clubhead is moving close to 130 miles per hour. The ball will zoom away at nearly 100 miles per hour. Think about *that* the next time someone shouts *Fore!*

Our sport instructional guides are bestsellers
because each book contains hundreds of images, is
packed with expert advice and retails for a great
price. No one else comes close.

"Start-Up Sports® tackles the hottest sports.
Forthright. Simple."
— Library Journal

Check out our entire catalog at trackspublishing.com

Tracks Publishing
140 Brightwood Avenue
Chula Vista, CA 91910
800-443-3570
tracks@cox.net

Tracks books are available through all major
booksellers — in stores and online.

trackspublishing.com

Start-Up Sports®

Doug Werner is the author or coauthor of all 11
books in the *Start-Up Sports®* series. He lives in
San Diego, California with his wife, Kathleen,
and daughter, Joy.